ANCESTRAL VOICES

Religion and Nationalism in Ireland

CONOR CRUISE O'BRIEN

POOLBEG

Published in 1994 by
Poolbeg Press Ltd,
Knocksedan House,
123 Baldoyle Industrial Estate,
Dublin 13, Ireland

A catalogue record for this book is available from the British Library.

ISBN 1 85371 429 1

Cover painting: *Shillelagh Dreaming – Stonehead* by Micky Donnelly
Cover design by Poolbeg Group Services Ltd
Set by Poolbeg Group Services Ltd in Garamond 10.5/13.5
Printed by The Guernsey Press Company Ltd,
Vale, Guernsey, Channel Islands.

For Owen Dudley Edwards

ACKNOWLEDGEMENTS

Thanks to Kitty and Maurice Quinn, for their patience, cheerfulness and skill, in bringing order out of the chaotic scrawl of my manuscript.

Thanks to Kate for initiating the project, and for the pleasure of co-operating with her, in bringing it to fruition.

Thanks to Maire, for working closely with me, on several drafts of the text, and for making the final version a great deal better than it would otherwise have been. Since we were married, thirty-two years ago, every book of mine has benefited from her co-operation, this one perhaps most of all.

Thanks to Owen, whose vigilance in the detection of historical and literary errors matches that of his hero, Sherlock Holmes, in the detection of crime. See Dedication.

Thanks to Vinnie Doyle, Gerry Mulligan and Marianne Heron of the *Irish Independent* and to Aengus Fanning, Anne Harris and Willie Keily of the *Sunday Independent* for kindly enabling me to reach large audiences in Ireland (South and North) regularly with messages closely related to that of *Ancestral Voices*.

Thanks to Andreas Whittam-Smith, Mary Dejevsky and Jane Taylor, for kindly giving me similar opportunities to reach a significant section of British public opinion.

Thanks to Bob Connor, Kent Mullikin and my colleagues at the National Centre for the Humanities, North Carolina, for enabling me to begin work on *Ancestral Voices* in a delightful environment and in distinguished, congenial and stimulating scholarly company.

Thanks to my oldest friend, Patrick Lynch, from whose wisdom I have been benefiting since we first met in the Department of Finance of Ireland fifty two years ago.

Thanks to Jack and Doreen Brennan, Frank Callanan, Brian

Barret, Eoghan Harris, Gerry Gregg, Sheila Iremonger, Dennis Kennedy, Bob McCartney, Maire and Muiris MacConghail, Tony Moriarty, John A Murphy, Tommy Murtagh, Maire Walshe and Father Michael O'Neill for increasing my knowledge of Ireland, North and South, and for the pleasure of their company.

Thanks, finally to Donal and Rita and Sarah; to Fedelma, Nicholas, Lawrence and Mark; to Kate (again) and Joe and Ali, and to Patrick and Margaret; and Maire again. For being who and what they are, to my constant joy.

I am sometimes asked whether I feel "isolated" presumably because my views on things like Ancestral Voices are not everyone's cup of tea. I don't feel in the least isolated. I live and move in the best of company.

FOREWORD

In 1986, I delivered a series of four lectures on religion and nationalism: the Massey Lectures, at Harvard University. The lectures were later published by Harvard University Press (1988) as *God Land: Reflections on Religion and Nationalism.* To simplify the thesis considerably, *God Land* is about the mutual historical interactions of religion and nationalism, in the Judeo-Christian culture – especially in Europe and North America. Nationalism and Christianity have been interacting, and often converging, over many centuries, despite the uncompromising efforts of Jesus and the early Christians to separate religion from all attachment to territory.

Kate Cruise O'Brien, on behalf of Poolbeg Press, has encouraged me to pursue this line of thought in *Ancestral Voices*, through Irish history from the Penal Laws into our own time. I do so the more willingly because my interest in the general subject matter has derived mainly from my family's share in the specific Irish experiences of the workings of these formidable world-historical forces.

The form which my education took, in the Ireland of the twenties and thirties, was largely the result of a quite paradoxical interaction of religion and nationalism. I was educated mainly at Sandford Park School, Dublin and Trinity College Dublin. Both these institutions were of Protestant ethos and, in politics, of unionist tradition, though the latter was becoming recessive, in the new State.

But a main reason why I was attending these schools was

1

that Irish nationalism, with its roots in the Catholic community (to which my family belonged) was impelling me in the direction of something very like its opposite. My first cousin Owen Sheehy-Skeffington, nine years older than myself, had attended Sandford Park and Trinity College, and I was following in his wake. Owen's mother had sent him there. Hanna was a widow. Her husband, a noncombatant, had been taken as a hostage, during the fighting of Easter Week, 1916, and shot by firing squad on the order of a British officer, Captain Bowen-Colthurst, subsequently charged with murder, and found guilty but insane.

Hanna became an active and prominent member in the fervently nationalist Republican movement, and she actively supported the Republican side in the Irish Civil War (1922-3). The Republican side was condemned by the Catholic Church, and its leaders excommunicated. Catholic schools were under the control of the Catholic hierarchy, responsible for these decisions. Hanna, therefore, decided not to send Owen to a Catholic school. The only other schools were of Protestant ethos, but not doctrinally committed to any particular political position over the Irish Civil War.

I doubt if Hanna felt particularly attracted to the Protestant ethos, but she preferred it to its alternative: a conservative authoritarian Catholic education with an anti-Republican slant.

There were other forces at work, in the choice of schools, as far as I was concerned. My father had been an agnostic, a child of the eighteenth-century Enlightenment, and he preferred Protestant (or post-Protestant) education to a Catholic one, because the Protestant tradition is more open to Enlightenment. But if my father's inclination had not been supported by Hanna's attitude and Owen's example, I doubt if I could have gone down that road. (My father was taken seriously ill at the time when the decision was taken).

Owen and I found ourselves in what was (considering our Catholic and nationalist ancestry and traditions) a somewhat exotic educational environment. We both took to it well, and I believe we both owed a lot to it. But it was important to observe certain taboos. We might have broken with the Catholic Church, but there must be no question of a break with Irish nationalism. God Save the King and the Loyal Toast were part of the culture in which we now found ourselves, but we must have no truck with either of these anti-national symbols: we must register our rejection by sitting down for both. Owen did, and I followed suit. Our teachers, both at Sandford and Trinity, tolerated these mild acts of defiance. They were not really important to any one else but ourselves, but to us they were important. They represented a kind of lifeline to the Nation. An exiguous one, I agree, but meaningful at the time.

My preoccupation with interactions of religion and nationalism begins right there. The preoccupation is evident, for example, in the subject-matter and treatment in my first two books, *Maria Cross* (1952) a study in the Catholic imagination, and *Parnell and his Party* (1957). I was never a Catholic, doctrinally, but I was always curious about Catholicism, and both attracted and repelled by it. For most of my life, I was less curious about Irish nationalism than about Catholicism and much more inclined to take nationalism for granted. All my family were Irish nationalists, though of different shades, and I vaguely felt myself to belong in there somewhere, culturally, and almost genetically. There is a comfort in shared assumptions and since I could not share the theological assumptions of my neighbours, it was all the more important to share the nationalist ones, if in their milder and more diffuse forms. Let me quote here two paragraphs from my autobiography, now in progress. This is from the second autobiographical excerpt, which appeared in *The Atlantic Monthly* in June 1994:

"So when Owen and I went to those Protestant schools, were we then turning into unionists? Certainly not! was Owen's determined answer, fervently echoed by me. Perish the thought! Somewhere in there, at the levels of the psyche I am trying to explore, was the notion that religion and nationality were like lungs. One lung was gone: it might aptly be described as past praying for. But if you lost the other one, you would be finished.

"Fortunately for us, perhaps, there were rituals available through which we could bear witness to our continuing faith in the nation. Ireland (that is, the twenty-six county state) was still technically a dominion of the Crown, complete with a governor-general, under the Anglo-Irish Treaty. Of course no proper nationalist would sing 'God Save the King' or stand for the loyal toast. But unionists (alias Protestants) were free to do so, and did. At Trinity College, Owen sat down for 'God Save the King' and the loyal toast. In due course I followed suit. The dons were less disapproving than I expected. Owen had broken the ice. The family penchant for sitting down at the wrong times had been established. Also we were in Protestant eyes Catholics by inheritance if not by theology, and therefore knew no better.

"For most of my life – fifty-four years of it indeed – I did not seriously question what Irish nationalism was about. I was led to do so when the offensive of the Provisional IRA began in 1971. This was, and is, a major convergence of religion and nationalism: a Catholic and nationalist offensive, not only (as claimed) against a British occupation but against the Protestant and unionist population of Northern Ireland: a kind of Holy War. In the autumn of that year I attended the annual conference of the Irish Transport and General Workers Union in Galway. There was a resolution down for the release of Republican prisoners. I saw this as collusion with the Provisional religious-nationalist offensive, and therefore I publicly opposed it, from the Conference podium, to the anger of the other delegates. There began a commitment to challenge all forms of collusion with those forces; a commitment which has continued now for twenty-three years."

Let me quote a final autobiographical excerpt.

"It is a bit disconcerting for me now to see how strong the pull of Irish nationalism had been throughout my life. Since 1971 – the beginning of the Provisional IRA offensive – I have been known in Ireland, where I now live, as top *anti*-nationalist. I have addressed the Friends of the Union – the Union, that is, of Great Britain and Northern Ireland. You can hardly get further away from Irish nationalism than that, many people hold.

"Yet I claim an underlying consistency and continuity. I was brought up to detest imperialism, epitomised in the manic and haunting figure of Captain Bowen-Colthurst, who murdered my uncle Frank Sheehy-Skeffington during the Easter Rising. As a servant of the United Nations, I combated a British imperialist enterprise in Central Africa in 1961: the covert effort to sustain secession in Katanga in order to bolster the masked white supremacy of the then Central African Federation. From 1965-1969, in America, I took part in the protest movement against an American imperialist enterprise: the war in Vietnam. And from 1971 until now I have been combating an Irish Catholic imperialist enterprise: the effort to force the Protestants of Northern Ireland, by a combination of paramilitary terror and political pressure, into a United Ireland that they don't want. I addressed the Friends of the Union to show solidarity with that beleaguered community against the forces working against them within my own community. And I suppose my Protestant education has something to do with that solidarity.

"I doubt whether Hanna would accept that continuity. But Owen would. He died in 1969, before the Provisional IRA offensive began. But he had made known his uncompromising hostility to earlier IRA efforts in the same direction. So when I first spoke out against the Provisional IRA and its accomplices, in the year the Provisional offensive began, 1971, two years after Owen's death, I had the inner certainty that we were at one on this. And that certainty still sustains me."

GHOSTS

And mid that tumult Kubla heard from far
Ancestral voices prophesying war.
          Coleridge, *Kubla Khan*

"A living man is certain to stop talking.
But once a dead man begins calling out (instead of keeping
quiet as is usually the case) – who is to silence him?"
          Søren Kierkegaard (1813-1855)

"*Mrs. Alving*: I just have to pick up a newspaper, and it's as if
I could see the ghosts slipping between the lines".
          Ibsen, *Ghosts* (1881)

"Here be ghosts that I have raised this Christmastide, ghosts of
dead men that have bequeathed a trust to us living men.
Ghosts are troublesome things, in a house or in a family, as
we knew even before Ibsen taught us. There is only one way
to appease a ghost. You must do the thing it asks you. The
ghosts of a nation sometimes ask very big things and they
must be appeased, whatever the cost."
          Patrick Pearse, Christmas Day, 1915

ANCESTRAL VOICES

RELIGION AND NATIONALISM IN IRELAND

Q. Have the Irish preserved the faith preached to them by St Patrick? A. Yes; the Irish have ever been conspicuous for their devoted attachment to the faith from which not all the horrors of persecution nor the blandishments of proselytism have been able to separate them.

Catechism of Irish History (1876)

"In the martyrology of history, among crucified nations, Ireland occupies the foremost place." – *Sinn Féin* (ed. Arthur Griffith) 29 March 1919, Article, "Nationality".[1]

These two quotations represent the combination of Catholic and nationalist ideology systematically inculcated by the Irish Christian Brothers, and less regularly encouraged by a number of others (not all of them of Catholic background) in the nineteenth and early twentieth century. As an article by a past pupil published in the late nineteenth century put it: "The Christian Brothers school is the hearth of a holy patriotism".[2]

Note that the *Catechism of Irish History* quoted above assumes that "the Irish" means Irish Catholics, and nobody else. This assumption has been very strong in the Irish Catholic culture, not only in Ireland, but throughout the

---

1. *Sinn Féin* is quoting from a French publication *Gazette Franco-Britannique*, attacking the British for having excluded the Sinn Féin party from the Versailles Peace Conference. I believe the French publication got this idea from Maud Gonne. She is on record as being a devout believer in "Crucified Nation"(see p. 133) and was the principal propagandist for the Irish nationalist cause in Paris from the late nineteenth century to 1917.

2. Article "Voices from the Past" cited in Barry M Coldrey's seminal work, *Faith and Fatherland: The Christian Brothers and the Development of Irish Nationalism, 1838-1921* (Dublin, 1988), p. 126. In general the contribution of the Irish Christian Brothers to Irish education has been enormous and to a great extent positive. But the nature of my subject restricts me, in this essay, to a consideration of their ideological role.

English-speaking world, in the United States, Canada and Australasia. It has been carried, not only through Catholic schools – among which the Christian Brothers are only the most indefatigable and explicit carriers – but above all in millions of Catholic homes. Even today, the assumption that the Catholics are the only real Irish shapes the attitudes of many Irish-Americans to Northern Ireland. It is also worth noting that this has been *official* Catholic doctrine. *The Catechism* was issued with the highest ecclesiastical approval under Cardinal Cullen.

To a significant extent, the modern Irish State is the product of that ideology, not only in general but specifically of the form inculcated by the Christian Brothers. Patrick Pearse and six others out of the fifteen men executed immediately after the Easter Rising of 1916 were past pupils of the Brothers, as were many of the rank and file, in that Rising and in the hostilities of 1919-21. The two leaders who dominated the first thirty years of the new State – WT Cosgrave and Eamon de Valera – had also been pupils of the Brothers.

The Irish Catholic-nationalist ideology harks back, essentially, to the Irish situation as it had been at the end of the seventeenth century.

The decisive battle of Aughrim, in 1691, had brought to an end the Irish section of the European religious wars which raged from the late sixteenth to the late seventeenth century. In those wars, Ireland had been a focus of international attention, to the misfortune of its inhabitants. Beginning with James Fitzmaurice Fitzgerald in the 1570's, Irish rebels – whatever their individual motives for rebellion – appealed for support to the Pope and the European Catholic powers. The Reformation Crown was illegitimate in the eyes of the Pope, and consequently the English (and later the British) monarchs felt they could not trust those of their subjects who owed religious allegiance to a Pope who was releasing them from their political allegiance to their Monarch. It was in consequence of this dangerous situation that James I – following a counsel of Machiavelli's – did his best to supplant subjects he could not trust, in favour of subjects he could trust. In Ireland, this meant replacing Catholics by Protestants: the policy pursued by James in the Plantation of Ulster in the first decade of the seventeenth century. The Plantation, mainly in Central Ulster, met with only partial success, but a parallel private enterprise process of land-purchase, mainly by Scottish Protestants, around the same time, in Antrim and Down, was more effective. The settlers differed from the (partly) supplanted natives not only in religion but also in language, culture and degree of technological development. The relations between those two communities, from the early seventeenth century on, have a striking resemblance to those between Jews and Arabs today, from Jordan to the sea and thereabouts. Everywhere in Ireland, by the end of the seventeenth century, religious and political allegiance tended to coincide, and in Ulster they coincided almost absolutely.

Throughout Ireland, the Catholics, comprehensively defeated in war, and suffering the political, legal and economic consequences of defeat, necessarily experienced a sense of solidarity that extended far beyond their common religious affiliations. Ethnic origins – as, for those formerly known as Old English – simply ceased to be important. What was coming into being was an Irish Catholic nation. Irish Catholics, the great majority of the people of the island, had been proscribed as Catholics, and also felt themselves to be oppressed as a nation. Ethnically they were an amalgam of *Gaedhil* (Gaels) and *Gaill* (foreigners). The old *Gaill* were descendants of Scandinavians, Scots and Welsh, Hiberno-Normans, and English settlers of the fifteenth and sixteenth centuries, with much intermarriage between the different stocks, as well as traditions of rivalry and intermittent hostilities between them. But the Irish Penal Laws took no legal cognizance of ethnicity, only of religious affiliation; they bore down on all Irish Catholics, irrespective of ancestry. Those who were oppressed for professing a common religion – Gaedhil as well as Gaill – came to feel a common sense of nationality, which they do not seem on the whole to have experienced before. Indeed, works in the Irish language by Hiberno-Roman Counter-Reformation clerics, like Keating and Hackett were strong contributing factors in this outcome.

Programmatically, the Catholic Church did not, in the period of the Penal Laws, and for some time thereafter, encourage political nationalism. Indeed, the Church actually sought to discourage expressions of nationalism, seeing these as a barrier to the long process of dismantling the Penal Laws, a process which lasted, roughly, from the last quarter of the eighteenth century to the second quarter of the nineteenth. During this period, defenders of the remaining Penal Laws argued that Catholics could not safely be entrusted with political rights, since their religion required them to reject the legitimacy of the Protestant Crown, and was therefore subversive of the political order, and favourable to the designs of Britain's external enemies. This objection appeared decisive up to 1766, the year in which Pope Clement XIII withdrew Papal recognition from the House of Stuart. Henceforward, Catholic spokesmen, including Bishops, could and did plausibly argue that the British Monarch would have no more loyal subjects than the Irish Roman Catholics, once their religious disabilities were removed. The mood of the Enlightenment, in late eighteenth-century Britain, also favoured the removal of such disabilities, as outmoded vestiges of an age of superstition and bigotry. This conjuncture, together with the pressures of the American Revolution, led to the first measure of Catholic emancipation: the Catholic Relief Act of 1778, masterminded by Edmund Burke in the British House of Commons.

Throughout the American Revolution, Catholic Ireland was quiet, and Catholic spokesmen contrasted what they presented as the loyalty of their people, with the many manifestations of Irish Protestant sympathy for the revolting colonists. In this period, we can occasionally hear the voices of Catholic nationalism, in Gaelic poems celebrating British defeats in America. But the official spokesmen of Catholic Ireland – the Bishops and the surviving Catholic landlords –

were careful to confine their public statements to the need for redress of religious grievances and, within that context, to stress their loyalty, and that of their people, to the Crown. That the people felt anything closely resembling loyalty to George III may reasonably be doubted, but they showed no recorded signs of rejecting or resenting the policy, or the tactics, of their Bishops.

In the century 1690-1790, there are few recorded signs of nationalism among Catholics, and the leaders of the Irish Catholics are repudiating nationalism in favour of political assimilation, following religious emancipation. In the 1790's however, under the impact of the French Revolution, Irish nationalism asserts itself for the first time, among Irish Catholics, as a force distinct from official Catholicism, and partly in conflict with the latter. Yet at a deeper level, the new Revolutionary nationalism appears to have been continuous, emotionally, with the older religious nationalism of the Counter-Reformation.

There are all sorts of difficulty here, both technical and more than technical. Technically, both the Counter-Reformation and the version of Republicanism that spread out from Revolutionary France are international ideological movements, transcending nationalism. Also, Counter-Reformation and Revolutionary Republicanism are widely – even wildly – different, conceptually speaking. Yet in Ireland the same sort of people who were moved by the religious ideology in the sixteenth and seventeenth centuries, were moved by the irreligious one in the eighteenth, without ceasing to be moved by the religious one, as well.

Cognitively, all this is almost too complicated to bear. Yet emotionally it is quite easy, and nationalism is an emotional force, though it sounds like an ideology. It happens that, in my teens, I saw this preposterous transition reenacted before my eyes. This was at a historical Military Tattoo in Dublin, circa 1930. At the relevant point, we saw first the soldiers of the mid-seventeenth-century Confederation of Kilkenny, under the classically Counter-Reformation banner: *In Omni Tribulatione et Angustia Spes Nostra Jesu Ac Maria* with immediately after these the Jacobite Catholics of the late seventeenth century, quite an understandable succession. But the next in line were United Irish rebels of 1798, bearing Wolfe Tone sloganry about the Common Name of Irishman, Catholic, Protestant and Dissenter. The audience seemed able to take this in their stride, as familiar to their traditions. Both sets of participants in the pageants were felt, I believe, to be good Catholic nationalists, despite discrepant banners, the first set of which did not appear to be nationalist while the second set was nominally nondenominational.

In retrospect, the two sets of movements appeared to be continuous, and indeed there was always an emotional continuity between them. But in terms of their relationship to the authority of the Catholic Church, the two were very different. Whatever nationalism was present in the Confederation of Kilkenny, and in the support for James II, was of a kind countenanced and encouraged by the Catholic Church in Ireland as well as by Rome. But the revolutionary United Irish movement of the 1790's which contributed to the great insurrection of 1798, was condemned by the Catholic Church, both internationally – from the Pope down – and in Ireland by all the Bishops, and the great majority of the clergy at every level. This was the first great rift, since the sixteenth century, between the institutional Church (as we would now put it) and the nationalist sentiments of Irish Catholics.

THE CHURCH AND THE REPUBLIC

Modern Irish Republicanism, as authoritatively defined by Patrick Pearse, claims descent from Theobald Wolfe Tone and the "United Irish" rebels of 1798.[3] Because these were condemned, and the Catholic rebels excommunicated, by the Church, there have been tensions, and fluctuations in tension,

---

3. In the nineteenth century, Protestant Young Irelanders admired Tone, but Catholic nationalists in the same period seem to have fought shy of him, perhaps more because of his suicide than because of the general condemnation of the 1798 Rising by the Church authorities. For guidance on this point, as on many others, I am indebted to Owen Dudley Edwards.

between the Church and the Republican Movement – and therefore between religion and nationalism – for nearly two hundred years now. The tendency in the late twentieth century, however, is towards increasing convergence.

Throughout the nineteenth century, and into the twentieth, the Republican movement ascribed the Hierarchy's condemnation of the United Irishmen and the 1798 Rising, to the subservience of the Hierarchy to the British Government, partly as a result of Papal connivance with British power. This interpretation, while not altogether without relevance, leaves out of account the main ideological and international forces involved. The United Irish movement, in its revolutionary phase (from 1795 on) looked for and obtained the support of revolutionary France. And the French Revolution was hostile to Catholicism. The Catholic Church, both internationally and in Ireland, had therefore solid doctrinal and institutional reasons, different from those of Britain, for opposing the French Revolution. And in Ireland, opposing the French Revolution meant opposing the United Irishmen. So confrontation between the two forces, religion and nationalism, was inescapable at this time.

It was not, however, a simple confrontation. The insurrection of 1798 was not just the work of the United Irishmen, with their putatively oecumenical and genuinely Jacobin ideology. It was also – and possibly to an even greater extent – the work of the Defenders, a specifically Catholic agrarian secret society, originating from the sporadic conflicts between Catholics and Protestants in those parts of Ulster where adherents of the two forms of Christianity were found (as they mostly still are) in approximately equal numbers; and inheriting a blood-feud.

In theory, Defenderism and the United Irish movement were poles apart. Defenderism was luxuriantly sectarian, the United Irishmen were anti-sectarian. The Defenders were Catholic, millenarian nationalists. The United Irishmen were *Irish* nationalists; religion had nothing to do with the matter, in United Irish theory. And nothing could be more remote, in theory, from the dark ages of millenarianism, than the original ideology of the United Irishmen: a flower, not merely of the Enlightenment, but of the most advanced phase of the Enlightenment, in the world-emancipating decrees of the French Revolution, beginning with the Declaration of the Rights of Man and of the Citizen, in August, 1789.

These distinctions were clear to the United Irishmen, in their reformist phase (before 1793) when they would have no truck with the Defenders (any more than with the Protestant opposite numbers of the Defenders). In that phase, the United Irish Movement was one of educated, middle-class radical reformists, some of Protestant background, some of Catholic, but all strongly influenced by the Enlightenment, and thus more like one another than they were like most of their Protestant and Catholic contemporaries. But as the movement became revolutionary, and went in quest of mass support, its meaning changed. Enlightenment took on incongruous millenarian overtones. There is a strong millenarian note in all revolutions. But in the French Revolution (as later in the Communist and Nazi ones) the millennium was a secular one: a new set of doctrines entirely superseding all religious ones and creating an Earthly Paradise, for the secular faithful.

In Ireland, however, where supernatural religious faith was far more firmly rooted than in the great European centres, the secular version of the millennium became inseparable from older supernatural ones. For United Irishmen of Protestant origin this was doubly difficult. The millenarianism of their Protestant kinsfolk – which was quite widespread – was specifically and ferociously anti-Catholic, replete with references to the Whore of Babylon. There could be no question of a nationalism that could incorporate Enlightenment, Catholics and *that*. But nor could enlightened Protestants accommodate themselves to a Catholic millenarianism that looked forward, not to the superseding of religion in general, but to the specific extirpation of Protestant heresy. Protestants (or post-Protestants) took part in the insurrections of 1798, but the Protestant insurrections were distinct from the Catholic ones and the Catholic ones took an anti-Protestant turn. The often uneasy, but remarkably durable, blending of religion and nationalism, was an affair of Catholics.[4] It had existed long before the United Irish movement, outlasted it and is still at work.

Once the revolutionary ferment began, the United Irish movement, in Catholic Ireland, merged with its theoretical opposite, the Defenders. The Catholic Church (as an institution) did its best to discourage the Defenders who, though far from enlightened, were a sort of heretics. The Church knew that the French Revolutionaries were militantly anti-Catholic, but the Defenders believed that the same French Revolutionaries were God's chosen agents in bringing on the Catholic millennium. A Defender catechism, said to have been circulated on the eve of the 1798 Rising, survives. It runs in part:

"'Are you *concerned*? I am. To what? To the National Convention. What do you design by that cause? To quell all nations, dethrone all kings and to plant the true religion that was lost at the Reformation. Who sent you? Simon Peter, the head of the Church.' Signed by order of the Chief Consul."[5]

A striking feature of the Defenders' identification of Catholicism with the French Revolutionary cause was the Defenders' use of the scapular. Scapulars, to which miraculous powers were attributed, had been a feature of popular piety, as part of the cult of the Blessed Virgin, since the thirteenth century. As used by the Defenders, they remained holy and miraculous but were *also* revolutionary symbols. The rector of Lacken, James Little, in his diary recording events in Mayo during the French invasion, pointed to the use made of scapulars and confraternities by the radicals in mobilising the

---

4. On the Protestant side, there was a partially-similar and nearly symmetrical association of religion and political allegiance; usually in resistance to Catholic nationalism. See the writings of Professor ATQ Stewart, especially *The Narrow Ground*. But the specific blend of religion and nationalism, in Ireland, was and is peculiarly Catholic.

5. Quoted in Thomas Bartlett, "Defenders and Defenderism in 1795", Irish Historical Studies (1985, p. 375)

people: "after undergoing the cookery of scapularism," he declared, the people were allowed to feast upon "the dish of atheistical libertinism".[6]

The Church authorities took alarm at this development: In the west, the Archbishop of Tuam, James Little, published a pastoral against scapulars which he believed had not only become objects of superstition, but had been used as banners by the rebels.[7]

The Church officially condemned the Rebellion, and all the Bishops and many of the clergy sincerely abhorred it. Yet there are signs of ambivalence: the relation of the Catholic clergy as a whole to the Rebellion is a complex matter. Daire Keogh, in his most illuminating study, *The French Disease*, sums up as follows: "In the frantic political activity of the period, it was impossible for the clergy to remain aloof from the concerns of the people and many of their number willingly became involved in the political process, allowing the occasions afforded by their profession to be harnessed in the cause. This was despite the strenuous exertions of the prelates. Yet, in the militant preparations which culminated in the 1798 rebellion, only a few dozen priests sided with the United Irishmen. The vast majority adopted positions of non-involvement or of loyalty to the government."[8]

A curious incident related by Keogh shows, however, that traces of Counter-Reformation "Holy War" theology subsisted in the institutional Church even through the French Revolutionary period. One of the most senior members of the clergy who had taken part in the 1798 Rebellion was Myles Prendergast, the Augustinian Prior of Murrisk. Prendergast was captured after the Battle of Ballinamuck but escaped, killing a prison guard in the process. Keogh: "John Rice, assistant general of the [Augustinian] order – whose brother, Edmund founded the Irish Christian Brothers – applied to Propaganda

---

6. Daire Keogh, *The French Disease: The Catholic Church and Radicalism in Ireland, 1790-1800* (Dublin, *Four Courts Press*, 1993) p.124
7. *French Disease*, p. 125
8. *French Disease*, pp. 134-5

on Prendergast's behalf for a dispensation for killing the prison guard. This was granted on the understanding that the dead man was a Protestant, but once it emerged that he had killed a Catholic the decision was reversed and the case referred to the Holy Office."[9]

The theoretical gulf which existed between what remained of the United Irish ideology and the mental and spiritual world of the Defenders was bridged in rough and ready ways during the 1798 Rising. Protestants were welcome, provided they joined the Revolution. If they did, they could be assigned nominal positions of leadership within it, as was the case with Bagenal Harvey in Wexford. If they did not, and most of them did not, the Catholic United Irishmen and their Defender allies could butcher them with an easy conscience. The Protestants who were piked to death on Wexford Bridge met this fate, not (at least in theory) because they were Protestants, but because they were counter-revolutionaries.

Precisely the same principle is asserted today by the Provisional IRA in their war against the Protestant and unionist inhabitants of Northern Ireland. "We have nothing against Protestants, as such . . . " is the watchword. As the people they actually are, with the full panoply of commitments they actually hold, the Provos have enough against them to murder them. And unfortunately, this point of view is not entirely confined to the ranks of active members of the Provisional IRA. I shall come back to that.

After the bloody suppression of the bloody Rising of 1798, the parameters of explicit Catholic nationalism were determined, for most of the nineteenth century, by the Catholic Church, whose authority appeared to be vindicated by the horrors of the insurrection and its repression. The Church had predicted the worst, and warned people in vain, and the Church had turned out to be right. So the Church was in the chair, for most of the century, though with growing uneasiness, in its second half.

9. Keogh, *French Disease*, p. 184

The Church supported the Act of Union in 1800. Some Catholics, including the young Daniel O'Connell, opposed the Act of Union. But outside Dublin city – where the end of the Parliament meant the loss of various kinds of employment – there can, in the nature of the case, have been little tendency to mourn the passing of an exclusively Protestant institution. If, as Pitt intended, the Union had been immediately accompanied by the completion of Catholic Emancipation, it is possible that Ireland would have come, in time, to accept its participation in the United Kingdom much in the way that Scotland still accepts it. That is to say that the Irish could have been part of the United Kingdom as the Scottish nation is, and with similar rumblings of nationalist uneasiness. The Catholic Church, if Pitt's original plan had been fulfilled, would have thrown its redoubtable weight onto the scale of a United Kingdom, in which Catholics had equal rights from the beginning. As Daire Keogh puts it ". . . In the absence of Catholic emancipation the Act of Union contained a fatal flaw which eventually transformed the Catholic question into the Irish question".[10]

As it was, the completion of Catholic Emancipation had to wait for more than a generation, and then was secured only as a result of a huge mass agitation led by Daniel O'Connell, fully supported by the Church, at every level. That the struggle for Catholic Emancipation had nationalist as well as religious implications was not doubted at the time and was demonstrated when O'Connell, immediately after Emancipation, took up the cause of Repeal of the Union. The Church approved of Repeal, in theory, but did not throw its full weight behind that nominally secular cause. After Emancipation, the Church could live with the Union, without pretending to love it.

Towards the mid-century, when the memory of the reality of 1798 had faded and a glorified and sentimentalised version of the Rising took its place, the Church's power to edit, as it

---

10. *The French Disease*, p. 217

were, Catholic nationalism, began to be challenged. Nationalist Protestants were part of that challenge. In Eastern Ulster, where most of the Protestants were, Irish nationalism had lost, for all but a tiny minority of Protestants, whatever charm it had had, after 1798 and Wexford Bridge. Almost all Ulster Protestants were by now unionists, as they still are. And so were most Protestants in the rest of Ireland. But a minority of intellectuals, of Protestant stock, saw in nationalism a potential bond with the mass of those among whom they lived. For some among them, this was also an opportunity for political or cultural leadership. There have been analogous developments in other cultures. Thus, in the late-nineteenth and early-twentieth century, Christian Arabs took a lead in the creation of Arab nationalism. In the Arab world, Christians were *ipso facto* excluded from the Muslim *UMMA*: the Consensus of the Faithful. So they sought to create a *political Umma*, a nationalist one, in which they could play a leading part.

The *ulema*, interpreters of Islamic law, never cared very much for Arab nationalism. Nor did the Catholic Church care very much for the nationalism of Young Ireland, in which Protestants like Thomas Davis were too active, and which looked back with too much favour on the United Irish movement of the previous century. By asserting a rigid separation between religion and politics, these nationalists were creating a distinct political sphere, resistant (in the Irish case) to the authority of the Church, which was held to be irrelevant to politics. In that sphere (as Churchmen saw it) the Protestant intruders could mingle with disloyal Catholics: dangers of mixed marriages there, and also of political mischief. In the nature of the case, the intruding infidel – the Irish Protestant or Christian Arab – is liable to be more extreme in his or her nationalism than the Catholic or Muslim. It is a way of asserting leadership, and of disrupting the traditional consensus of the Faithful, Catholic or Muslim.

Young Ireland, as a specific movement, faded with the ignominious failure of the Risings of 1848, in the wake of the

Great Famine. But the tensions represented by Young Ireland continued to trouble the Church throughout the second half of the nineteenth century and first quarter of the twentieth. This was not exactly a tension between religion and nationalism; though it often appeared to take that shape. The Church remained basically nationalist (though generally not separatist) and Irish nationalists remained overwhelmingly Catholic. But there was a tension between the Church and manifestations of nationalism that were regarded as hazardous, illicit, slanting over into disobedience, disbelief, indifferentism in religious matters, and even Protestantism.

CARDINAL CULLEN: MANAGER OF NATIONALISM

So how was the Church to deal with the potentially subversive force of resurgent Irish nationalism? It was the powerful ingenious and politic mind of Paul Cardinal Cullen (1803-1878) which found a satisfactory way of countering the danger. Cullen was Archbishop, first of Armagh and then of Dublin, over a period embracing nearly thirty years, from 1849 to 1878. Cullen is thought of as archetypically anti-nationalist. Well he was, especially in Italian affairs, and he was also archetypically Irish Catholic nationalist, which is what makes him fit so snugly into the ambivalent and ambiguous culture we are discussing. Monsignor Patrick J Corish has summed up Cullen's position on *nationalism* with admirable succinctness: "Cullen was intensely Irish, but his patriotism, in marked contrast with, say, that of Thomas Davis, rested on a complete identification of Faith and Fatherland: his interpretation of past history, which is the basis of all patriotism, was dominated by the fact of Irish attachment to the Catholic faith."[11] Cullen led the Church in excommunicating and isolating the leaders of the revolutionary Fenian movement – heirs of the United Irishmen – in the 1860's and 1870's. Not all

---

11. 'Corish, Cardinal Cullen and the National Association' in *Reactions to Irish Nationalism* with an introduction by Alan O'Day (Dublin, Gill and Macmillan, 1987), p.127

the clergy, and not even all the Bishops, were happy about the severity towards the Fenians, as letters to the Rector of the Irish College in Rome, William Kirby, in the 1860's show. Father James O'Leary, a teacher at St Colman's College, Fermoy wrote to Kirby, about the Fenian rising: "It is an uprising of the Irish race against Saxon domination. There is no 'irreligious tendency' in it, no matter what may be said . . . Would to God they could smash the first heretical power on the globe and destroy the great bulwark of the devil."[12] Father O'Leary's Bishop Dr William Keane, took a similar line. He wrote to Kirby: "The mass of the people, down to the very children going to school, are either Fenians or sympathise with the Fenians, not because they wish to give up the faith or neglect their religious duties, but because they hate England, the enemy of their country and of their creed, and of our Holy Father and of everything Catholic, and because the Fenians are opposed to England."[13]

Cullen did not relent in relation to the Fenians, but he managed to put the blame for Fenianism on to Protestants and "irreligious nationalists" in general. As he wrote to Cardinal Barnabò, Prefect of Propaganda: "What is certain is that almost all the leaders of Fenianism have been educated in the Protestant Dublin University, in the Queen's Colleges and in the normal and [denominationally] mixed national schools. The youth of the Christian Brothers schools, of the Catholic colleges, and of the Catholic university, have not been compromised".[14] Emmet Larkin comments: "While Cullen's *ex parte* statements about Fenianism certainly need to be taken with a large grain of salt, he did apparently sense what was really at stake for the Irish Church in the Fenian conspiracy. The Fenians were in their quarrel with the Church attempting to drive a nationalist wedge between the clergy and the people, and Cullen was determined that this was to be resisted at all costs."[15]

---

12. Quoted in 'Corish, Cardinal Cullen' etc. p. 121
13. Quoted in Emmet Larkin, *The Consolidation of the Roman Catholic Church in Ireland, 1860-1870* (Dublin, Gill and Macmillan, 1987), p. 415
14. Quoted in Larkin, *Consolidation* etc. p. 423
15. Larkin, *Consolidation* etc. pp. 423-4

The condemnation of Fenianism was the negative aspect of Cullen's strategy for resisting the insertion of that wedge. The positive aspect was the encouragement of a fervent Irish nationalism which was also specifically and fervently Catholic. Cullen became the supreme and indispensable supplier of fuel to the "hearth of holy patriotism" kept aflame by the teaching of Irish history in the Christian Brothers' Schools.

This was a great watershed in the history of religion and nationalism in Ireland. Hitherto – since the defeat in the religious wars – the Church had officially tended to discourage expressions of nationalism. Now the Church was officially inculcating religious nationalism in order to keep the irreligious kind in check.

By the late 1860's, in the wake of the Fenian Rising of 1867, some of the British establishment were beginning to worry about the Christian Brothers' teaching of history, and where it might be leading. During the proceedings of the Powis Commission inquiry into primary education in Ireland in 1868, one of the Commissioners, Judge William Brooke, questioned Cullen about the Brothers' history textbooks. The tendency of Brooke's questioning appears in the following passage from his subsequent minority report:

"Professing to cultivate a spirit of Irish nationality, the Christian Brothers have compiled for their more advanced pupils reading books abounding in narratives of English perfidy and cruelty, and many passages in prose and verse of such a character that the Irish student can hardly fail to be imbued with a detestation of any connection with England. The danger of such a political education is the more to be apprehended because the Roman Catholic clergy . . . seem wholly unconscious of the danger referred to."[16]

Cullen's response is summed up as follows by Barry Coldrey:

"Cullen had also approved highly of the Christian Brothers' *Historical Class-Book* and did not see why it should be criticised simply because it had been written for Catholics and

16. Coldrey: *Faith and Fatherland* pp. 129-30

not for Protestants. Even though the book mentioned facts 'certainly not creditable to the English Government', he did not think that it promoted hostility. His reasoning was that if the children did not learn these facts under men such as the Christian Brothers, who taught that we were not justified in hating those who wronged us, they would learn them from newspapers. He maintained that the textbooks inculcated the Catholic faith, which taught charity to all men and respect for the established government. 'Faith thus being strengthened . . . tends to preserve a spirit of subjection and obedience in the people.'"

Considering the inflammatory nature of the Brothers' teaching of Irish history, this 'defence' is almost contemptuous in its perfunctory sophistry: a combination of qualities familiar enough in Irish episcopal public statements in the nineteenth and twentieth centuries. But Cullen was a most sagacious Churchman, in relation to the consolidation and expansion of Catholic power. He certainly knew what he was doing, though he was not about to explain it to a British Commission (or to any body of laymen). The key to what may appear as contradictory in the Cardinal's approach is contained in words quoted by Manning's biographer, Purcell, in which Cullen vehemently attacks "the revolutionary and *irreligious* (my italics) Nationalists of Ireland".[17]

Cullen and the Hierarchy, and the Brothers with their approval, were aiming to supplant irreligious nationalists, especially Protestant nationalists, with religious ones, meaning obedient Catholic ones, and they were singularly successful in this. One of the reasons for this was that Catholic nationalism, as offered by the Brothers, was simpler, more exciting and more relevant than the cumbrous and complicated doctrinal baggage inherited by the Republican Movement from a bygone intellectual age in Irish history. The French Revolution was dead and gone. Enlightenment oecumenism had no attraction for a healthy Irish Catholic boy. On the other hand Catholic nationalism made for exciting history lessons: Good

---

17. Purcell *Life of Manning*, ii. p. 610

versus Evil; heroic Irish Catholics defending their kind against the bottomless and inexplicable malevolence of English Protestants. And Protestant and English were interchangeable terms. Just as the Penal Laws presumed no such person as an Irish Catholic to exist, so the ideology of the Christian Brothers, fully countenanced by the Hierarchy at this time, presumes no such person as an Irish Protestant to exist. (see the passage from *Catechism of Irish History* quoted at the outset.) And this attitude, in more diluted forms, is widespread today among Irish Catholics.

The actual course of Irish history from the late sixteenth century to the end of the eighteenth, provides abundant material for history lessons of this kind. All you have to do is to leave out the atrocities committed by your own side, and provide copious details of those committed by the enemy. Thus Protestant historians exaggerated the atrocities committed by Catholics against Protestants in the rebellion of 1641, and minimised or justified the massacres of Catholics by Cromwell's forces eight years later. Catholic historians pounced on the Protestant exaggerations of 1641, and ignored, or played down the Catholic atrocities which had actually occurred. Cromwell's atrocities, on the other hand, got from Catholics the kind of attention Protestants devoted to 1641. All political and religious zealots everywhere do this kind of thing instinctively. The Christian Brothers were exceptional only in that, through them the pedagogic resources of a powerful and efficient (and, in some ways exemplary) religious order became committed to this type of historiography, inculcating it into generations of their pupils, with the blessing of the Irish Catholic hierarchy.

In the years between the suppression of the Fenian rising of 1867 and the First World War, the Church handled nationalism with the constructive ambiguity of which Paul Cullen had set the example. At one level, constitutional nationalism was encouraged. From 1886 on, the Hierarchy endorsed Home Rule: that is, local autonomy within the Empire. The Hierarchy had its own imperial leanings; this was a period during which there was much talk of Ireland's Spiritual Empire. This was, of course, something infinitely superior to Britain's Material Empire, but terrestrially, the two had a marked tendency to overlap. In Africa and Asia, the Spiritual Empire operated mainly within the territorial confines of the material one. Irish Catholics (in the Colonial and Indian services) helped to govern the material one, with no sign of clerical disapproval. And Irish Catholic nationalists, elected with the help of the Church, sat in the Imperial Parliament, and sometimes held the balance in it, throughout the heyday of the Empire, in the late nineteenth and early twentieth centuries. The Catholic Church, both in Ireland and in the Empire, benefited in many ways from their presence.

All that may seem a long way from the world of the Irish Christian Brothers, but it really is not. The constitutional nationalists, when on the hustings, appealed to the same folk-memory as the Brothers did, and so spoke a similar language. The upmarket religious orders, such as the Jesuits, and other Orders drawing their pupils from the upper sections of the middle class, prepared pupils for the spiritual and material Empires, but the distinction between them and the Brothers was one of function, rather than policy. The Jesuits were preparing their people for responsibility, which meant compromise, the capacity for nuance. The job of the Brothers – as broadly envisaged by Cardinal Cullen and his colleagues – was to keep the lower orders within the bounds of orthodoxy, by showing Irish nationalism and Catholicism to be inseparable, thus keeping irreligious nationalism at bay. Nuances were not the business of the Brothers. The upmarket Orders would see to those, and the Hierarchy was the ultimate arbiter of the whole system in which both the Brothers and the upmarket Orders had their appointed parts to play.

I referred earlier to Irish nationalists elected with the help of the Church. This was literally so from 1882 to 1914. By reason of a compact reached between Charles Stewart Parnell and the Church authorities, after the so-called "Kilmainham

Treaty" between Parnell and Gladstone in May 1882, the Catholic clergy, in each electoral district, became *ex officio* part of the National League, the grassroots machine of the Irish Parliamentary Party, under Parnell's leadership. Thus there was a formal institutional linkage, which was also a close working partnership, in this period, between religion and nationalism in Ireland. Specifically, between the Catholic Church and Constitutional Nationalism.

THE PARNELL SPLIT
O'SHEA VERSUS O'SHEA AND PARNELL

The Divorce Court crisis of 1890 and its bitter political and social consequences in 1891 disrupted this partnership, but only partially and temporarily. Institutionally, the Church-and-State working partnership, which had been built into the National League, by Parnell himself, remained in being. Only now, ironically, it was turned against its creator and helped to destroy him, in the three ghastly by-elections which Parnell lost in 1891.

Retrospectively, and especially in the eyes of writers and intellectuals, the Parnell Split came to be seen as a conflict between Irish nationalism and the Catholic Church. That was how Parnell himself presented it, and how his most devoted followers saw it. Most Irish nationalists, whether lay or clerical, genuinely didn't see it that way at the time, and they had a point. In terms of nationalist policy, there was no difference between the two sides. Parnell had entered into partnership with the clergy, on constitutional nationalist grounds, in 1882, and the partnership had been satisfactory to both sides until the Divorce Crisis introduced issues from outside the world of politics.

The view of the Parnell Split as a conflict between religion and nationalism is oversimplified. But the effects of the Split on the *relations* between religion and nationalism in Ireland were profound. The Split appeared (to some) to put the two forces on a collision course, but its longer-term effect was to bind them together more closely than ever. As Frank Callanan has demonstrated, in his brilliant and pioneering book, *The Parnell Split, 1890-91* (Cork UP 1992) what did most to break Parnell in 1891 was the fiery, scurrilous, ruthless, populistic Catholic-nationalism of Timothy Michael Healy. Many respectable anti-Parnellites (including my grandfather, David Sheehy) were disgusted by Healy's demagoguery. But it worked, and not just in those by-elections.

Essentially, though never quite explicitly, Healy's point was that Parnell was no fit leader for the Irish people (for "Irish people" as used by Irish Catholics, read always "Irish Catholic people") *because he was a Protestant*. Being a Protestant, he could not share the moral values of the Irish people, or understand how fiercely they resented any offence against chastity. Many priests were on hand to corroborate this view of the matter. But the most revealing aspect of the whole controversy was the unwilling testimony, in support of Healy's contention, supplied by Parnell's *defenders*. When cornered on the moral issue, these invariably suggested that, being a Protestant, Parnell could not be expected to understand, as a Catholic would, that adultery was wrong. None of them ever said this right out, but everyone knew that this was the theme of their hollow vague and barely coherent references whenever they were forced to allude to the abhorrent but all-pervading topic in the grisly year of 1891.

Since Parnell, there has been no Protestant leader of Irish nationalism, nor has any Protestant, ever since, been admitted to the inner circles of Irish nationalism. Token Prods only, like Muslims in Congress India. (The ceremonial office of President has been held by Muslims in India, and by Protestants in Ireland).

It is often suggested that the authority of the Catholic Church suffered as a result of its exercise in the Parnell split. It may have suffered, but not very much. The people whose authority was severely damaged were the constitutional nationalists, whose charisma left them, along with the leader they had had to leave. The relationship between the Church and nationalism was also altered, in some complex ways.

Specifically, the relationship between the Church and the constitutional nationalists was damaged. This was partly because the constitutional nationalists had declined in public esteem and were, in consequence, less valuable as allies. But it was also because a greener form of nationalism – Parnellite nationalism, markedly anti-clerical in the early 1890s – was making its presence felt in Dublin, especially among the young and among intellectuals. This was a new and particularly virulent strain of the "irreligious nationalism" so feared by Cardinal Cullen. Some account of all that had to be taken by the Church. The need was increasingly felt for a special kind of nationalist politics: one that would be as enthusiastic, as charismatic and anti-British as Parnellism, but shorn of the latter's anti-clerical and potentially antireligious elements and tendencies. In short, what was needed was militant *Catholic* nationalism. And this was precisely the need that the historical ideology of the Christian Brothers had been supplying, in the education of the young. Catholic nationalism was now needed, however, not only in the schools, but in the political arena, especially in cultural politics.

So it is not surprising that pupils of the Christian Brothers, steeped in their brand of nationalism, should come into the ascendant in the new balance of forces that took shape, once the immediate shock of the Parnell Split was over.

It took some years, but certainly no more than a decade, for that shock to wear off. In the early 1890's, relevant circles in Dublin (though not in rural or small-town Ireland) were in a mood to welcome the cultural nationalism of WB Yeats. They welcomed it in those days not only for its aesthetic and sentimental charms, but *because* it was a form of nationalism disapproved by the Church authorities, who had just murdered Parnell (according to the assumptions prevailing at the time in the circles in question). The Church disapproved of Yeats because he was a Protestant or worse, if worse there were. So bully for Yeats! The Church disapproved of "mixed" cultural activities, because these might lead to mixed marriages or worse, if worse there were. So what? One might just go ahead and marry a Protestant and be damned, to show those people what you felt about them murdering Parnell! Well, maybe not go so far as *that*! But there was a delightful frisson in declining to avoid authoritatively-designated occasions of sin, and this lent sexy spice to the whole Protestant-inspired cultural-nationalist enterprise. Paris was no doubt a wickeder city than Dublin in that same *fin-de-siècle*, but I doubt whether those Parisians enjoyed their wickedness nearly as much as our Dubliners enjoyed their not very *dangereuses liaisons*, of the heyday of Parnellite cultural nationalism, circa 1892. I regard this short episode as a kind of oasis in my sombre subject matter, and I am sorry now to be obliged to leave it and get back to the sombre, though even amid the sombre, there are diverting interludes.

With the dawn of the new century, Parnellism was on the shelf politically speaking. The Irish Parliamentary Party came together again in 1900, now for the first time under a Catholic leader. (The founder of the Party, Isaac Butt, had been a Protestant, as was his successor, Parnell). The new leader, John Redmond, claimed to inherit the mantle of Parnell, but his followers could be comfortably sure that no new Mrs O'Shea would come wrapped up in that mantle, this time round. Redmond was a good Catholic, and good family man.

The ranks of the constitutional nationalists were now closed. But by the same token, religion and nationalism were now converging again after a fairly short period of partial, but occasionally sharp, divergence. The Church and the reunited Party decided to bury the Parnell hatchet, and this was undoubtedly to their mutual advantage. But the burial of the Parnell hatchet had uncomfortable implications for the oecumenical version of cultural nationalism offered by Yeats and Lady Gregory and their Abbey Theatre. It was Parnellism that had won their access to Catholic audiences in Dublin and had made their work "politically correct" in that city, for the best part of a decade. But by the middle of the first decade of the new century, Parnellism was no longer *à la mode*, even in

Dublin. James Joyce has recorded its decay, and incipient demise, in "Ivy Day in the Committee Room."

PARNELLITE DUBLIN RECONQUERED

To say that the first decade of the twentieth century witnessed the recapture of Parnellite Dublin by the Catholic Church would be an over-simplification, though a suggestive one. Even at the height of its Parnellism, in the early 1890s, nationalist Dublin had never ceased to be Catholic. And even in the 1900s, when Parnellism had ceased to be politically relevant, nationalist Dublin never ceased to venerate the memory of Parnell, although nationalist Dubliners, and other Irish nationalists, were by now referring to that memory with increasing circumspection. The reunification of the Irish Parliamentary Party – under the leadership of the former Parnellite John Redmond, with the former anti-Parnellite, John Dillon, as his deputy – meant that references to the Parnell split were now taboo.

With that politically salutary Act of Oblivion, there was no longer even the shadow of a suggestion (outside the tiny Republican minority of that period) that Catholicism and nationalism could be at variance. The Church gave its blessing to the reunited Party, and did not boggle at the fact that it was reunited under the leadership of a formerly refractory member of their flock, John Redmond. Redmond, for his part, never again referred in public to the Church's role in the destruction of Parnell. That a veil should be drawn over all that had been an implicit condition of his election to the leadership of the reunited Party.

As former Parnellites and former anti-Parnellites buried their hatchets at the turn of the century, the newly-reunited Catholic-nationalist Ireland began to be increasingly responsive to a new slogan, "Irish-Ireland". The slogan was the coinage of a brilliant and pugnacious journalist: DP Moran. Moran was intensely Catholic and intensely nationalist: a thoroughgoing "Faith and Fatherland" person, fully in tune with the basic ideology of the Christian Brothers, but recklessly idiosyncratic in his personal formulations of the same.

The characteristics of an Irish Irelander, as these were beginning to emerge in 1900 were as follows:

He (or she) is Catholic, preferably, but if not Catholic, then thoroughly deferential to Catholic-nationalists, on all questions relating to the definition and practices of Irish-Ireland. He or she is more earnestly nationalistic than other Irish nationalists, including the Irish Parliamentary Party, and most of its supporters. He or she may be either constitutional-nationalist or Republican. Most Irish Irelanders were constitutional nationalists, up to 1914, but critical of the parliamentary leadership and its press.

He or she is enthusiastic about the Irish language, not necessarily able to speak or write the language in the here and now, but actively engaged in learning it, or at the very least, deemed to be doing so.

He or she is passionately opposed to all forms of English influence in Ireland, including the playing of foreign games, such as cricket and rugby, and therefore supports the Gaelic Athletic Association. (Founded in 1884 the GAA has been described as "intensely Anglophobic and an organisation avowedly nationalist, ostensibly Irish and, crucially, church supported").[18]

He or she – especially she – is rigidly chaste, in accordance with the norms of chastity laid down by the Catholic Church, and is dedicated to the suppression of all public manifestations of unchastity, especially in the theatre.

That was how the general picture of Irish-Ireland looked around the turn of the century. But the picture was to become sharper, with more ominous features, after DP Moran had

---

18. WF Mandle "The IRB and the Beginnings of the Gaelic Athletic Association" in *Reactions to Irish Nationalism* pp 97-99. Michael Cusack the founder of the GAA was, like other fervent nationalists, visited by patriotic and other ghosts. "He stated that in a dream the assorted shades of Wolfe Tone, Napper Tandy, Thomas Davis, Kickham, Speranza and Famine had come to him braving leering fiends" (Mandle p. 94). Cusack was of course the original of "the Citizen" in *Ulysses*.

founded his weekly paper, *The Leader*. The first issue of *The Leader* appeared on 1 September, 1900, in the autumn of the year that witnessed the reunification of the Irish Parliamentary Party. DP Moran had an unusually keen sense of the *Zeitgeist*, and a journalistic flair far above the normal.

Moran may have had clerical backing for the foundation of his paper, and both his paper and his Irish Ireland movement had significant, if discreet, support from the Hierarchy. David W Miller makes an interesting comparison between the attitudes of the Irish clergy towards the Irish parliamentary Party, on the one hand, and Irish Ireland on the other:

"The need to allay English Protestant misgivings had led the [Irish Parliamentary] Party leaders to enunciate a broad, tolerant concept of Irish nationality. The independent Ireland for which they worked would be a nation of diverse creeds, in which the tradition of Swift, Grattan, Davis and Parnell [all Protestants] would be as highly revered as that of O'Neill, O'Connell, McHale and Davitt [all Catholics]. Though few nationalists actively engaged in politics would have taken issue with this definition of Ireland, a very different version of nationalist ideology was also in circulation in this period. For DP Moran, editor of *The Leader*, Ireland was above all a Catholic country in which Protestants would be made welcome, but only on Catholic terms . . . Priests voted for the Irish Nationalist Party, but the nationalism that captured their affections was to be found not in the columns of Hansard, but in the columns of *The Leader*.[19]"

The "broad tolerant concept of Irish nationality" was mainly for export. *The Leader's* straightforward Catholic nationalism went down better at home.

In the years of its heyday – 1900 to 1914 – *The Leader* was the most exciting thing in Irish journalism. That, in itself, might not have been saying all that much. But by any standards, *The Leader* was an exciting journalistic product: sharply written, hard-hitting, taboo-breaking, and animated by

---

19. Miller: "The Roman Catholic Church in Ireland: 1898-1918": in *Reactions to Irish Nationalism* [ed] Alan O'Day (Dublin, 1987) pp. 195-6

a well-defined sense of purpose. DP Moran was a committed journalist, if ever there was one. Putting it more concretely, he was a great hater. It would probably not be quite fair to say that Moran hated Protestants, but it would be very near the truth. As Moran himself saw it, his mission was to subvert what remained of Protestant Ascendancy by putting the fear of God into the minority in Catholic Ireland.

The old citadel of Protestant Ascendancy – the power of Protestant landlords over Catholic tenants – had been obliged to capitulate by Gladstone's Land Act of 1881, brought about by Parnell, Davitt and the Land League, with strong financial backing from Irish Catholics in America. New legislation – mainly the Wyndham Act of 1903 – would remove the landlords from the scene altogether. The Local Government Act of 1898, democratising local government throughout Ireland, put such powers as local authorities possessed into Catholic-nationalist hands, in every part of Ireland, except Eastern Ulster, with its Protestant-unionist majorities. But formidable bastions of Protestant power and influence remained in urban life, especially in business and in education. *The Leader* now moved in on these bastions.

We are about to look at that sustained attack in some detail. But first let me set down my reason for giving *The Leader* so much attention, in the context of the present study. The reason is that the files of *The Leader*, from 1900 to 1914, constitute the only sustained explicit exposition of Catholic nationalism that we have. Throughout the eighteenth and nineteenth century, this whole area was generally covered by a fog of dissimulation and pseudo-oecumenism. After 1921, in the new Irish State, that decorous fog descends again and has never really lifted since. Today, that fog is so thick that we can't see where we are going, in relation to Northern Ireland and are in danger, in consequence, of falling into the pit of civil war.

The fog was generated in both main traditions of nationalism. The Republican tradition was dominated, in its formal ideology, and public expressions, by Wolfe Tone's

35

doctrine of the Common Name of Irishman obliterating, in theory, all political differences between Catholics, Protestants and Dissenters. So no proper Republican could ever give public vent in explicit terms to anti-Protestant feelings. The constitutional nationalists had more pragmatic reasons for an equivalent inhibition. They needed to play down the sectarian tendencies among their supporters in order to convince their English Liberal allies – most of whose followers were English Dissenters – that modern Catholic nationalism was part of the tolerant Enlightenment. Some of it actually was: both John Redmond and John Dillon were genuine liberals. Other Catholic nationalists were not, and few if any of the Catholic Bishops were. But it had suited all the constitutional nationalists, up to around 1900, to strike a tolerant and oecumenical note, as the Irish Parliamentary Party continued to do and as the nationalist daily press, in the service of the Party continued to do.

Under these conditions, DP Moran's acute professional eye had spotted a window of opportunity for an *independent* Catholic and nationalist weekly. *The Leader* would be broadly, though never uncritically or sycophantically, supportive of the reunited Parliamentary Party, and it would be militantly Catholic. But it would not be, and would not sound like, an official organ of either Church or Party. In this way, neither Church nor Party would have to take responsibility for anything the paper might say, which could give offence to English people or Protestants. *The Leader* was speaking for itself, and only for itself.

This left *The Leader* free to say many things which the nationalist daily press – the *Freeman's Journal* and the *Independent* – were not free to say, and which many Catholics and nationalists were delighted to hear. It also left *The Leader* free to adopt a refreshingly abrasive tone, markedly distinct from the boringly emollient tone to which the nationalist daily press was constrained by the necessities of pragmatic oecumenism.

In short *The Leader* could say out loud what other Catholic nationalists had been bottling up, or ostensibly repudiating, in public, for many generations. In the first decade-and-a-half of our century, those repressed feelings came gushing out, in the columns of *The Leader*. Putting it another way, in that period and in that paper, we have an opportunity to look at Catholic nationalism with the lid off. (Not that all Catholic nationalism is like this, but a great deal of it is, and is normally screened from public view). It was an opportunity that had never been presented before, and it was never to recur. So let us look at the files of *The Leader*, a lode exceptionally rich in the particular ore we are concerned to investigate.

THE GREAT TWIST OF THE SOURFACES

The Leader started out quietly enough, on what was soon to become the most strident enterprise in the history of successful Irish journalism. The first issue, on 1 September, 1900, carried a welcome for the new weekly, from WB Yeats. Yeats, addressing DP Moran, referred to "the many attacks you have made upon me and the movement I represent." This was a reference to attacks Moran had made on Yeats' *Countess Cathleen* (1892). These attacks were specifically Catholic, without any specifically nationalist rationale. Cardinal Logue had condemned the play – without either reading it or seeing it – on strictly theological lines and Moran followed suit. But the attacks fell flat. At this period, Dublin was still strongly Parnellite, and Yeats's Parnellite credentials were impeccable. If anything, an attack on Yeats's play by the head of the Catholic Church in Ireland tended to strengthen Yeats's position in Parnellite Dublin at this time. There was nothing objectionable in the play from a purely nationalist point of view, in so far as such a thing existed. Countess Cathleen is an Irishwoman of exceptional, if eccentric, virtue. Her chastity is above suspicion, and this characteristic deprived the Cardinal's theological strictures of the strongest relevant source of emotive power. Catholicism and nationalism, under these special conditions, failed to converge.

Yeats, despite that old difference of opinion, welcomed *The Leader* on general cultural-nationalist grounds, especially for its commitment to the objectives of the Gaelic League, and the revival of the Irish language. Yeats appeared anxious, for the sake of his theatre, to be accepted by the organ of Irish-Ireland, as an Irish-Irelander. Moran had presumably solicited Yeats's letter of approval and he replied to it in a conciliatory vein (8 September, 1900). It seemed like a burial of hatchets on both sides, but it wasn't. Moran, as the sequel would show, was keeping his own hatchet well-oiled and sharp, and ready for Mr Yeats.

It was not until its sixth issue, on October 6, that *The Leader* made its first appearance in the role of a journal of attack. Moran had no doubt learned from the failure of his polemic against *The Countess Cathleen*. His target this time was exquisitely well-chosen: the immorality of British stage productions in Ireland, in such places as the Gaiety Theatre, Dublin (leading commercial theatre). Catholic and nationalist minds were in happy unison about this one. Catholic Bishops had already publicly condemned such plays for their immorality. Nationalists were delighted to join in, but stressing the *British* origins of the immorality in question. "Most of the heroines of modern British drama are prostitutes."[20] This statement appeared under a rubric which was to be a regular one in *The Leader*: "The English Mind in Ireland". Actually, the particular play *The Leader* happened to be attacking was not originally a product of the English mind at all. The play was called *Zasa* and it was an adaptation from the French; its first success in the English-speaking world was in the United States. But it was being staged in Dublin by an English company and that was enough. Irish nationalists were not interested in French or American depravity, only in the English kind, and they were very interested indeed in that.

The *Zasa* affair was useful to *The Leader*, both ideologically

---

20. The words "British Prostitutes" had a satisfactory Catholic-nationalist resonance. Tim Healy had described Parnell's widow, in the week after her husband's death as "this British prostitute".

and commercially. The Catholic and nationalist daily press were not protesting against shows like *Zasa*, though the Bishops had condemned these. *The Leader*, by leading this attack, established itself as more Catholic than the *Freeman's Journal*, as well as more zealously nationalist. This was a healthy combination in early-twentieth-century Dublin. *The Leader* soon acquired a satisfactory volume of Church-related advertising. A typical issue, by the time *The Leader* was well-established (17 September, 1904) carried advertisements from the Catholic Truth Society; the Convent of St Louis, Monaghan; Dominican Convent, Galway; St Colman's College, Fermoy (all with columns of exam results); Convent of Our Lady and Charity of Refuge, Magdalen Asylum, Gloucester St; Parochial Church of St Columba, Drumcondra (Bazaar) and St Joseph's Seminary, Clondalkin; and related ads for altar candles, vestments etc. No informed Irish person of the period could glance down those columns of ads without realizing that *The Leader* stood high in the favour of the Irish Catholic Hierarchy. Implicit favour only, but that was enough.

By no coincidence, the principal target of *The Leader's* polemics was the Protestant community in Ireland, stigmatised as "Sourfaces" (a coinage of Moran's). The first salvo of that kind was fired by *The Leader* on 9 February, 1901 in an article sarcastically entitled "A Sad Day" and dealing with Irish people in mourning for Queen Victoria. Contemplating those mourners, *The Leader* mused:

"There is something very distinctive about the face of the average loyalist, it is characteristic in its way as that of a Jew. . . They all understand one another especially when employment is to be given. These brick-complexioned and sourfaced whole and part foreigners rule the country."

(*The Leader* was not any more anti-semitic than many other publications in Britain and Ireland in this period. But it wanted to tap anti-semitism for anti-Protestant and anti-British purposes, as in a reference to "Jewman Bull" (*Leader*, 26 July, 1902). When anti-semitic riots broke out in Limerick in 1904, *The Leader* denounced the Protestant Bishop of Limerick, Dr

Bunbury as "a bigot". The way in which the Bishop's bigotry had manifested itself was by protesting against the Limerick antisemites, who were Catholics. See *The Leader* 23 April to 4 June, 1904. "Bigots", in *The Leader*, invariably means Protestants).

From 1901 on, references to Sourfaces are a standard feature of *The Leader*, often in the form of apparently casual asides like the following, delivered in the course of an attack on the principal nationalist newspaper, the *Freeman's Journal*, for carrying advertisements of "low places of entertainment". In closing that theme *The Leader* added: "What the other papers had we don't know and are not interested in, let the Sourfaces look after their own".

The reference here is to the Protestant-and-unionist *Irish Times* of that period.

George Russell ("AE") and TW Rolleston are known to have protested against the use of crude sectarianism in the name of "Irish Ireland", and possibly some Catholic readers did as well. Moran's defence, in *The Leader* for 11 May, 1901 is unusually equivocal, for him. It runs:

"If a man is in doubt whether he is a Sourface or not let him look in the glass: if two men or women are in doubt let them look at one another. These are not infallible tests, for as a man may smile and smile and be a villain, so a man may smile and be a Sourface. A Sourface is not a Protestant, or a toy Atheist or a Unionist. A Sourface may be any of these things. It very often happens that a Sourface is a Protestant, or professes to be one; but he is not a Sourface because he is a Protestant, but because he is somethings else besides."

That was the official version. In reality, in the columns of *The Leader* "Sourface" always refers to Protestants, never to Catholics. The terms of reproof that apply to Catholics are "shoneen" and "West Briton". "Shoneen" is the harsher of the two epithets: it is generally used of what were also called "Castle Catholics": Catholic unionists. "West Briton" is a mildly derogatory term, applicable indeed to Sourfaces and shoneens, but including also many political nationalists, not yet fully-paid-up members of Irish Ireland. The upmarket Catholic schools – for example Clongowes, the Jesuit boarding-school and Belvedere, the Jesuit day-school – were West British in a number of ways, notably in playing "foreign games". But many products of these schools read *The Leader*. "West Briton" is telling these readers to mend their ways. If they start learning Irish they will be readily acceptable in what *The Leader* called "the new order in Ireland" (1 December, 1900). (They only need to *start* learning Irish). "Sourface" is something else: referring to a genetically-transmitted condition, and so almost beyond remedy. *Almost*. Moran allows that some Protestants can possibly be saved, nationally speaking, in a sort of a way:

"We want to go back to the Gael, the matrix of the Irish nation. If the Gael is to be raised, the proper place for the sympathetic Palesman is behind the Gael until he becomes absorbed. But it would appear that the price of the tolerance and of the alliance is that the Gael speaks under his breath and says 'Thank you' when one per cent of the former graciously smiles on him. Ireland has two religions and the majority cannot talk about their religion above their breath, for fear of appearing bigoted, intolerant and offending our patronizers." (*The Leader*, 5 January, 1901)

"Palesmen" in the context, means Protestant. A Protestant, it seems, can be saved only if he becomes absorbed. That is to say, he must become either a Catholic-nationalist or – at the very least – a loyal adherent, at a subordinate level, to a form of nationalism entirely defined and dominated by Irish Catholics.

That form of absorption remains the nightmare of Ulster Protestants, and is at the root of their resistance to being incorporated in a united Ireland.

The classic formulation of *The Leader*'s fusion of Irish Catholicism and Irish nationalism is contained in an article "Faith and Fatherland" (8 June, 1901). In this Moran laid it down:

"There was a time in Ireland when public opinion was

Irish; it was then Catholic as well. That was when the Irish Gael lived freely and in honour in his own land. And the faith which he intertwined with patriotism was the traditional Catholic faith handed down to him from Patric. Meanwhile the alien colony became firmly rooted in the land and tried to totally extinguish every vestige of Irish Ireland – and almost succeeded. Aliens in race, and mostly aliens in religion they tried to plant their religion, language, in a word their whole civilization on the conquered country [and on] the Native Irish as distinct from the alien settlers."

Year after year, in every issue, *The Leader* kept up its campaign against the alien race. Moran had a name for the campaign. It was called, "The Great Twist of the Sourfaces". Any complaint about The Great Twist was entered under the rubric "The Great Whine". Complaints about intimidation or ill treatment of Protestants in the rural areas were dealt with as part of The Great Whine. In rural areas boycotting and intimidation of "Soupers" were fairly widespread. Soupers were individuals and families who had been Catholics but had become Protestants, supposedly to obtain food ("soup") or other material benefits in famine times. *The Leader* dealt as follows with Protestant complaints about an incident involving a priest and a souper in Limerick. "A Catholic priest is guilty of the crime of saying, 'This is a Souper house, this is a souper house, this doctor is a souper doctor, no Catholic is to go in there'"! (6 July, 1901).

One gets quite often from the pages of *The Leader* a whiff of rural intimidation against Protestants, with sly editorial encouragement. But let me offer just one more example. *The Leader* (4 March 1905) quoted with approval a resolution of the Westport Urban Council:

"That we fear the Protestants of this district have created a serious state of affairs by not having spoken out strongly in repudiation of the audacious calumnies of certain Orange newspapers, that the lives and property of Protestants are unsafe in the South and West of Ireland, and that they are able to live in these parts only by effacing themselves . . . "

There is an exquisite irony there. *The Leader* was assiduous in telling the Protestants of Ireland to efface themselves, "stand behind the Gael", pending their eventual absorption into the Catholic nation. Yet when they did efface themselves, in rural Ireland, they were to find this was not enough. As well as effacing themselves, they must also "speak out strongly" against "the audacious calumny" that they were being required to efface themselves . . .

The Leader thought this provocative attitude on the part of the Protestants showed the need for "some sort of a Catholic Organization for the defence and assertion of their civil rights."

Just as black racists in modern America think that only whites can be racists, so *The Leader* thought that only Protestants could be bigots: "Why should Irish Catholics try to prove their tolerance when they have never been intolerant? Let those who have been intolerant prove that they have given it up" (*The Leader*, 31 May, 1902).

The significance of *The Leader*, in the context of our present study is that it constitutes a sustained declaration of the identity of Irish Catholicism and Irish nationalism.

Formally, official nationalism during this period repudiated any such identity, as it still does. Catholicism was religion, and nationalism was politics, two quite separate things. A person's religion was his own private affair. Irish nationalism belonged to all the Irish. So said the Irish Parliamentary Party and the *Freeman's Journal* then, and also the Republicans, and so say Fianna Fáil and the *Irish Times* today (the modern *Irish Times*, bearing no political resemblance to the newspaper of the same name in the early 1900's, known to *The Leader* as "the Bigots' Dustbin"). Few Protestants believed the old official version, or believe the present one. And I think that many Catholic nationalists, in their hearts, don't believe it either. No such compartmentalisation occurs in the psyche. Concerning Catholic nationalism, the Christian Brothers and *The Leader* are much nearer to the truth than the official version is.

My Mother, my Aunt and James Joyce

The Leader was in no sense a marginal publication. It was the journalistic flagship of Irish Ireland. The chief characteristics of Irish Irelanders are identified. Most Irish Irelanders read *The Leader*. They didn't necessarily go along with Moran's sectarianism, but they showed no clear signs of objecting to it. And Irish Ireland was the culture of young-middle-class Catholic and nationalist Ireland in the early years of the new century. That culture is part of my own intellectual background, for my mother and father were strong Irish Irelanders. So also were my father's sister, Cathleen and her future husband, the novelist Eimar O'Duffy; so were my mother's sisters, Hanna and Mary Sheehy and their future husbands, Francis Skeffington, who married Hanna, when both took the name Sheehy-Skeffington, and Tom Kettle who married Mary, without benefit of hyphen. It was only later that each and all of those would fall foul of *The Leader* in their different ways.

My mother's credentials as an Irish-Irelander were unusually good. She was not merely deemed to be learning Irish. She had studied it seriously, including a long stay in the Aran Islands and she spoke and wrote it fluently. She had also a strong sense of mission about the language and its culture. Her sense of mission seems to have impinged quite sharply on James Joyce. My mother is the main model of Miss Ivors in Joyce's story "The Dead" (in *Dubliners*). From her exchanges with the principal character in the story, Gabriel Conroy, we can glimpse something of Joyce's uncomfortable relation to Irish Ireland early in the century. Miss Ivors is introduced in the following passage:

"Lancers were arranged. Gabriel found himself partnered with Miss Ivors. She was a frank-mannered talkative young lady, with a freckled face and prominent brown eyes. She did not wear a low-cut bodice and the large brooch which was fixed on the front of her collar bore on it an Irish device."

The editor of the Penguin Classics edition of *Dubliners* (London, 1992) annotates the words: "She did not wear a low-cut bodice . . . the large brooch . . . an Irish device" as follows:

"The Celtic Revival of the 1880's onwards encouraged the self-conscious adoption of Celtic design in fashions and costume jewellery. Individuals who espoused the separatist cause and the Irish Ireland movement were often notably puritanical in sexual matters, which may account for Miss Ivors' modest evening wear."

"The Dead" continues:

"When they had taken their places, she said abruptly: – I have a crow to pluck with you. – With me? said Gabriel. She nodded her head gravely – What is it? asked Gabriel, smiling at her solemn manner. – Who is G.C. answered Miss Ivors, turning her eyes upon him. Gabriel coloured and was about to knit his brows, as if he did not understand, when she said bluntly:

" – O innocent Amy! I have found out that you write for *The Daily Express* [Unionist newspaper]. Now, aren't you ashamed of yourself? – Why should I be ashamed of myself? asked Gabriel, blinking his eyes and trying to smile.

" – Well, I'm ashamed of you, said Miss Ivors, frankly. To say you'd write for a rag like that. I didn't think you were a West Briton.

"A look of perplexity appeared on Gabriel's face. It was true that he wrote a literary column every Wednesday in *The Daily Express* for which he was paid fifteen shillings. But that didn't make him a West Briton surely . . . He did not know how to meet her charge. He wanted to say that literature was above politics. But they were friends of many years standing and their careers had been parallel, first at the University and then as teachers: he could not risk a grandiose phrase with her. He continued blinking his eyes and trying to smile and murmured bravely that he saw nothing political in writing reviews of books.

"When their turn to cross [in the dance] had come he was still perplexed and inattentive. Miss Ivors promptly took his hand in a warm grasp and said in a soft friendly tone:

" – Of course, I was only joking. Come, we cross now.

"When they were together again she spoke of the

University question and Gabriel found himself more at ease. A friend of hers had shown her his review of Browning's poems. That was how she had found out the secret but she liked the review immensely. Then she said suddenly:

" – O, Mr. Conroy, will you come for an excursion to the Aran Isles this summer? We're going to stay there a whole month. It will be splendid out in the Atlantic. You ought to come. Mr. Clancy is coming, and Mr. Kilkelly and Kathleen Kearney. It would be splendid for Gretta too [Gabriel's wife] if she did come. She's from Connacht isn't she?[21]

" – Her people are, said Gabriel shortly.

" – But you will come, won't you? said Miss Ivors, laying her warm hand eagerly on his arm.

" – The fact is, said Gabriel, I have already arranged to go –

" – Go where? asked Miss Ivors.

" – Well, you know every year I go for a cycling tour with some fellows and so –

" – But where? asked Miss Ivors.

" – Well, we usually go to France or Belgium or perhaps Germany, said Gabriel awkwardly.

" – And why do you go to France and Belgium, said Miss Ivors, instead of visiting your own land?

" – Well, said Gabriel, if it comes to that, you know, Irish is not my language.

" Their neighbours had turned to listen to the cross-examination. Gabriel glanced right and left nervously and tried to keep his good humour under the ordeal which was making a blush inside his forehead.

" – And haven't you your own land to visit, continued Miss Ivors, that you know nothing of, your own people, and your own country?

" – O, to tell you the truth, retorted Gabriel suddenly, I'm sick of my own country, sick of it.

" – Why? asked Miss Ivors. Gabriel did not answer for his retort had heated him.

" – Why? repeated Miss Ivors. They had to go visiting together

---

21. Joyce's wife, Nora Barnacle, was from a Galway family

[a reference to a movement in the dance] and as he had not answered her Miss Ivors said warmly:

" – Of course, you've no answer.

"Gabriel tried to cover his agitation by taking part in the dance with great energy. He avoided her eyes for he had seen a sour expression on her face. But when they met in the long chain he was surprised to feel his hand warmly pressed. She looked at him from under her brows for a moment quizzically until he smiled. Then, just as the chain was about to start again, she stood on tiptoe and whispered into his ear:

" – West Briton!

"When the lancers were over Gabriel went away to a remote corner of the room where Freddy Malins' mother was sitting . . . Her voice had a catch in it, like her son's, and she stuttered slightly. While her tongue rambled on Gabriel tried to banish from his mind all memory of the unpleasant incident with Miss Ivors. Of course the girl or woman, or whatever she was, was an enthusiast but there was a time for all things. Perhaps he ought not to have answered her like that. But she had no right to call him a West Briton before people, even in joke. She had tried to make him ridiculous before people, heckling him and staring at him with her rabbit's eyes. Miss Ivors would not stay for supper.

– But how can you get home, asked Mrs. Conroy. – O, its only two steps up the quay. Gabriel hesitated a moment and said: – If you will allow me, Miss Ivors, I'll see you home if you're really obliged to go. But Miss Ivors broke away from them. – I won't hear of it, she cried. For goodness sake go in to your suppers and don't mind me. I'm quite well able to take care of myself. – Well, you're the comical girl, Molly, said Mrs. Conroy. – *Beannacht libh*, [bless you] cried Miss Ivors with a laugh as she ran down the staircase. Mary Jane gazed after her, a moodily puzzled expression on her face, while Mrs. Conroy leaned over the banisters to listen for the hall-door. Gabriel asked himself was he the cause of her abrupt departure. But she did not seem to be in ill humour: she had gone away laughing. He stared blankly down the staircase."

In a footnote, Terence Brown says that Hanna Sheehy "may have supplied the model for Miss Ivors". The most clearly identifiable characteristics, however, are those of my mother and not those of her sister Hanna. The physical description fits my mother, Kathleen Sheehy, and does not fit Hanna; my mother's eyes were dark brown, Hanna's pale blue. My mother was an Irish language enthusiast, and had spent time in the Aran Islands. Hanna did not know Irish at all, and would never have expressed enthusiasm for a language she hadn't troubled to learn. She was indeed an Irish Irelander, but primarily on the political and social side, not on the cultural and linguistic. The late Richard Ellman believed that my mother was the model for the character, and I think she was the main model. On the other hand, the aggressivity of the character, the cutting edge of that "cross-examination", is much more like Hanna than it is like my mother, who was generally known as "the nicest of the Sheehys". It seems possible that Joyce may have been conflating a memory of a conversation with Kathleen about the Irish language, with a memory of a conversation with Hanna, about politics. Certainly Hanna would have been *much* more likely than Kathleen to call a person a West Briton, "before people".

In his Introduction to *Dubliners*, Terence Brown says:

"The attempt to revive the Irish language receives short shift in Joyce's telling portrait of an enthusiast in the person of Miss Ivors in 'The Dead' all coquettish mischief-making and puritan ardour".

That is indeed how the episode must look to a person who has no sympathy at all with the movement to revive the Irish language or with Irish Ireland in any of its manifestations. This is also how it appears to some foreign Joyceans, looking down on Catholic and nationalist Dublin through, as they believe, Joyce's eyes. But these eyes are not really Joyce's. Joyce had been born and brought up in a Catholic and nationalist culture. He was fighting his way out of it, in both of its aspects, but he also felt the pull of it, in both its aspects. "The Dead" tells of how painful it was, at this time, for a person born and brought up as an Irish nationalist to tear himself away from Irish nationalism. Gabriel Conroy greatly resents the importunities of Miss Ivors, but he does not see either Miss Ivors or the movement she represents as contemptible. He respects Miss Ivors's intellect. When he thinks of saying something pompous to her he stops, with the reflection: "he could not risk a grandiose phrase with her". What she demands of him – commitment to Irish Ireland and to the Irish language – evokes feelings of dread, resentment and guilt, but not of contempt. He dislikes Irish Ireland, but he hates to be called a West Briton.

Through Irish Ireland, as through Irish Catholicism, Joyce hears ancestral voices calling. He knows them for siren voices and, like his model, Ulysses, he causes himself to be bound to the mast, lest he yield to them and drown. It was well for his art that he did so. He resisted them, not because he despised them as some of his modern admirers suggest, but because he feared their power over him. They were the voices of his own ancestors after all. As they are of mine.

MY FATHER AND THE GREAT TWIST

My father's commitment to Irish Ireland was as strong as my mother's, in those days. It was sufficiently strong indeed, to attract the, mostly favourable, attention of DP Moran himself early in my father's undergraduate career. *The Leader* in its issue of 15 April, 1905 reported on a paper read by Francis Cruise O'Brien to the New School of Literature and Drama in Ireland. This was a bit of an occasion in the Dublin of that day as the speakers included WB Yeats and George Russell (AE). *The Leader* commented: "Mr O'Brien is the coming man of the college . . ."

"The college" is the Royal University, which became, three years later, the National University of Ireland. "The college", as a Catholic and nationalist insitution – in ethos though not by statute – had the approval of *The Leader*, as against Trinity

College, always identified, in the columns of *The Leader*, as "the Sourface University". *The Leader's* reference to my father went on:

" . . . and his paper was a remarkable achievement for one only at the beginning of his student career; indeed, one's chief criticism would be that it displayed too open a mind, an undue capacity for harbouring intellectual positions necessarily in themselves opposed".

"The positions necessarily in themselves opposed" were those of Irish Ireland and the Irish Literary Movement; the relationship between the two is explored in the following section of this study.

My father became a fairly frequent contributor to *The Leader*, over the next five years or so. The relationship only began to deteriorate as the Woman's Suffrage movement began to gain influence, and arouse antagonism, in the second decade of the century. DP Moran hated Women's Suffrage as a West British fad. I think he even obscurely felt that it was part of a fiendish British conspiracy against the chastity of Irish womanhood. By July, 1912, *The Leader* was lampooning "Cruso" and his brothers-in-law, Tom Kettle and Francis Sheehy-Skeffington as the most prominent Irish males associated with the feminist cause. (*The Leader* assumed that the males involved must really be running the show). But by that time *The Leader* itself was nearing the end of its long ascendancy over Irish Ireland.

My father's contributions to DP Moran's *Leader* are something of a puzzle to me. I discuss the puzzle here because I believe an answer to it may have a bearing on the workings of Irish Catholic nationalism, and in particular on a versatile and potent phenomenon which I propose to call "differentials in the reception and resonance of ancestral voices."

The puzzle consists in this: My father as I knew him – that is about twenty years after the period considered in this section of the present study – was not a believing or practising Catholic, and he was an Irish nationalist of only the mildest description. As regards nationality, I learned from my father to be proud of being Irish, to be especially proud of being an O'Brien and most particularly proud of being an O'Brien of Ennistymon. As regards Catholicity, I learned to be proud that our ancestors had stuck to their religion in the centuries of persecution. That my father could no longer believe in the religion in question – at a time in Ireland (after 1921) when it had become advantageous to profess it – did not detract from his pride in the fidelity of his ancestors to it, in the days when such fidelity was extremely *dis*advantageous. Yet there was no suggestion whatever (either from my father or my mother) that we should or would bear a grudge against our Protestant contemporaries, because of what their ancestors had done to our ancestors. On the contrary, my father was much more at home with liberal Protestants (and post-Protestants) and "lapsed" Catholics, like himself, than he was with strongly-believing Catholics, such as my Aunt Mary, Tom Kettle's widow, and my father's *bête noire*.

These things being so, it was by my father's decision (supported and carried out by my mother) that I was sent to a non-denominational secondary school, which in the Dublin of those days meant a school of Protestant ethos. From Sandford Park School I went on, almost automatically, to Trinity College, Dublin and that is where the puzzle begins. In the terminology of *The Leader* Sandford Park was a Sourface School and Trinity College was the Sourface University.

So how could my father have been a frequent contributor to *The Leader* at a time when DP Moran's Great Twist of the Sourfaces was in full swing?

It is true that my father's contributions were by no means part of the Great Twist. They are altogether free from xenophobia or sectarian animosity. But the puzzle still remains. How could a person with my father's views, temperament, associations and inclinations make contributions, of any kind, to the Dublin periodical which was doing the most in those days to encourage xenophobia and sectarian ill-feeling?

One possible explanation is that Protestant Ascendancy was not only a recent memory, in the Ireland of those days, but a continuing fact of urban life. Dublin firms owned by Protestants openly discriminated against Catholics. Part of the Great Twist was the publication in *The Leader*, week after week, of advertisements from the *Irish Times*, stipulating "Protestants only". In fighting against that sort of thing, Moran would have had the support of all Catholics (including cradle Catholics, like my father). But of course Moran did not stop there. He was not so much interested in correcting abuses as in using them to generate hatred and ostracism of Protestants in general.

I believe the real answer lies in certain phenomena I have already referred to: the differential, the mental and moral ascendancy which fierce Catholic-nationalists tend to have over the milder kind. Those who hear the ancestral voices only faintly are to some extent in thrall to those who hear them loud and clear, calling for vengeance. Putting it another way, in terms of our epigraph, those who are dedicated to appeasing these ghosts have authority over those who would prefer, if left to themselves, to have as little as possible to do with the ghosts.

In my own family, in my youth, we all stood in awe of my Aunt Hanna, the only really implacable nationalist among us, and having always behind her the ghost of her murdered husband, Francis Sheehy-Skeffington. This conferred on Hanna a sort of penumbra of licence, covering almost anything she might do, in the line of ghost-appeasement. Thus, though neither my mother nor my father can have relished her verbal massacre of Sean O'Casey (see "Hanna and Séan," p. 122), they never objected to it, and continued to defer to her. I believe similar considerations probably operated with my father, in relation to The Great Twist. He must have found it a repellent, yet at a deeper level, legitimate response. DP Moran was obeying voices and appeasing ghosts. A person so engaged is not to be interrupted or challenged, by persons less confidently conversant with the agenda of the dead.

In the late twentieth century, the IRA draws on the same source of authority, over Catholic-nationalists of far milder description. I shall come back to that.

The differentials in intensity of Catholic-nationalism were apparent to my mother and father and their friends in the years from 1900 to 1914, but their lethal potential was undreamt of. They were confidently and joyfully preparing for an untroubled future in a Home Rule Ireland. They had no premonition of a blood-dimmed tide. The emotions that DP Moran, and nationalists more extreme than he, were playing on, within the Irish Ireland movement, must have seemed harmless to them and perhaps (to my father at least) a bit funny. The past was unhappy, but the future was bright. There was no conception that the past could reach out into the future and destroy people. They were uneasily aware of the ghosts, and deferential to them on occasion, but they had no idea of the extent of the power of the ghosts over the living and over those yet to be born.

I feel an overwhelming sense of pathos as I look back at the world of my parents, and of Frank and Hanna, and Tom and Mary, in the bliss of that false dawn:

All heedless of the gathering whirlwind's sway
Which hush'd in grim repose expects its evening's prey

WB YEATS AND OTHER NATIONALISTS

The relations between Irish Ireland, as represented by *The Leader*, and Yeats's Irish Literary Movement, make an interesting case-history in the interaction of religion and nationalism in the field of culture.

As we have seen Yeats had established himself in the Parnellite Dublin of the 1890's as the leading figure in a cultural-nationalist movement which came to be known as the Irish Literary Movement. The Church had viewed this development with suspicion and some apprehension. As we have also seen Cardinal Logue had condemned Yeats's

Countess Cathleen ni Houlihan (1892) but that specifically Catholic-theological attack had been fended off rather easily. DP Moran had been involved in that fiasco, as it was from a Catholic point of view. Moran was determined to try again in the more propitious atmosphere of the first decade of the new century. But Moran's sharp and bitter little mind could learn from its mistakes. This time, the line of attack would be, not just Catholic, but Catholic-nationalist. Yeats himself claimed to be a nationalist but *The Leader* would challenge the validity of that claim, with the potent counter-claim that Irish nationalism had to be Catholic, and so Yeats and his friends did not qualify.

Moran had a clear-cut and far-sighted strategy for reclaiming post-Parnellite Dublin for Catholic Ireland. His strategy was eclectic. From Parnellism Moran took over the virulent Anglophobia of the Chief's last year, and also (in a more muted form) the suspicion towards Irish parliamentarians, as possibly corrupted by living in Britain in cosy collaboration with English Liberals ("English Liberals" had been Parnell's line, but Moran would add "Protestants" to Liberals). The elimination of the anti-clerical component which had once dominated Dublin Parnellism was basic to the strategy of "reclaiming". But Moran was clever enough to avoid the error of replacing anti-clericalism by clericalism. The tone of *The Leader* was not sycophantic to the clergy, as the nationalist dailies of the period often were. The tone was one of independent judgement within the parameters of the Catholic faith. *The Leader* frequently criticised the upper-class Catholic schools, for West British tendencies, such as their addiction to foreign games. Even the Christian Brothers were gently chided for not being sufficiently committed to the teaching of Irish. The Hierarchy was never directly attacked but *The Leader* discreetly implied that some of the Bishops might not be fully living up to the ideals of Irish Ireland. All this was shrewdly calculated for the Catholic reclamation of post-Parnellite Dublin. People who had been anti-clerical in the 1890's could take *The Leader* in the 1900's, without feeling that they had capitulated to clerical dictation. The strategy seems to have been understood by those who were being gently criticised and whose influence *The Leader* was in fact restoring. The Catholic ads flowed in in satisfactory volume and *The Leader* flourished.

The elimination of Protestant influence from the nationalist cultural scene, was a prime objective of *The Leader*, within the grand strategy of Catholic nationalism. The chief target was WB Yeats, still popular among Irish Ireland people at the turn of the century. That popularity had to be broken. As we have seen *The Leader* in its first two issues staged what looked like a reconciliation between Yeats and DP Moran. But that was a feint on Moran's part. The attack began in *The Leader*'s issue of 24 November, 1900. Yeats was not named but the target was a Yeatsian enterprise: "an assembly known by the strange name: The National Literary Society".

What was strange about that name? The fact that the word "National" was being usurped by a society led by Protestants. *The Leader* went on: "We would point out that the West British way of looking at things may have been in keeping with the spirit of ten years ago, but though the 'National' Literary Society does not know it, we have advanced a little in the last ten years [i.e. since the Parnell Split]. Would it not be time they ceased talking nonsense in this society or else shifted it over to Birmingham?"

In the name of Irish Ireland *The Leader* is serving notice that Yeats's Irish Literary Movement is a West British Movement.

In response to that attack, a respected Protestant cultural nationalist TW Rolleston put two questions.

"Are Davis and Ferguson and Yeats and AE to be nothing to the Irish Catholic because he is a Catholic and are De Vere and Griffin and Morgan to be nothing to me because I am a Protestant?" (*Leader*, 5 January, 1901)

Without directly answering Rolleston's questions, Moran responded in the same issue with the declaration of principle beginning "We want to go back to the Gael . . . " Here, "sympathetic Palesmen" – that is, Protestant applicants for acceptance as nationalists – are notified of the conditions for their acceptance. Yeats and his friends (not named) are told their place is "behind the Gael" until they "become absorbed" into the Catholic nation. In the meantime they will be tolerated as apprentice nationalists, under instruction from Catholic sources as to what is really national and what West British. Not an easy prescription for Yeats to follow.

Even for some devoted Irish Irelanders, *The Leader*'s line on Yeats was already a bit much. Father J O'Donovan of Loughrea, a regular contributor to *The Leader,* wrote a gentle letter of protest which the paper published (12 January, 1901). The letter quoted *The Leader*'s verdict, "Even Mr Yeats does not understand us, he has yet to write one line that will strike a chord of the Irish heart". Commenting on this, Father O'Donovan offered "an instance to the contrary that struck me very much: I have a dainty volume of Mr Yeats's collected poems. One evening I missed my book from its accustomed place. I asked my housekeeper if she saw it. In some confusion she said it was in the kitchen where she had taken it to read one of the poems – The Ballad of Peter Gilligan – to a neighbour. 'To tell you the truth, sir, the two of us cried over it.'"

Ignoring the "instance to the contrary", *The Leader* kept up the pressure, and the pressure was beginning to hurt by the summer of 1901. Yeats wrote to Lady Gregory about a meeting with his publisher, AH Bullen: "Last Saturday and to my great surprise I met Bullen in Dublin . . . He told me that he was amazed to find the hostility to me of the booksellers – [name omitted] he declared, seemed to hardly like to speak my name. I am looked on as heterodox, it seems . . . Russell [George Russell, "AE"] told me that clerical influence was he believed working against me because of my mysticism. He accuses Father Finlay and his Jesuits of working behind Moran".[22]

Yeats and AE knew by now that they were up against

22. Yeats to Lady Gregory, postmarked 21 May, 1901, in Alan Wade, ed. *The Letters of W.B. Yeats* (London, 1954)

something but they seem curiously vague about its nature. In suspecting "clerical influence" behind Moran they are certainly right, in a general way, but only in a general way. The idea that "the Jesuits" as a concerted body were behind Moran is certainly wide of the mark. The Jesuits were under suspicion in Irish-Ireland circles for West British tendencies so that even their enemies could hardly suspect them of being so jesuitical as to be covertly prompting Irish-Ireland zealots. (The received wisdom of the time, however, was that "the Jesuits" "have someone for everything" and Father Tom Finaly SJ, is likely enough to have disliked Yeats's kind of poetry.) No-one, in any case was "behind" Moran in the sense – often used in Ireland – of controlling his activities. Moran represented a tacit alliance between the Catholic Church and the radical nationalists of Irish Ireland, but he wasn't being run by the clergy or by any section of them. His journalism is pungently individual; characteristics no institutional house-organ could ever posses.

The use of the terms "heterodox" and "mysticism" also suggest a failure to grasp the point. The booksellers were not frightened by "mysticism" or anything hoity-toity of that kind. What was frightening them was the label "West Briton." We have seen the suffering that label caused when "Miss Ivors" pinned it on to "Gabriel Conroy" about this time. The same label had now been affixed to Yeats by *The Leader*. And a Protestant would find the label harder to shake off than a Catholic would. A Catholic could get rid of it by certain relatively minor adjustments in his or her lifestyle. But a Protestant, once so labelled, was stuck with the label, genetically as it were. The more offensive term "Sourface" was conceived as racial, and applied in a racist manner. Not all Protestants, perhaps, were Sourfaces. But a Protestant identified as a West Briton, is certainly a Sourface. A West-British Sourface, claiming to be a nationalist, would be seen as a kind of spy, infiltrating the cultural citadel of Irish Ireland. So no wonder that booksellers had difficulty in speaking the name of WB Yeats in the summer of 1901.

I think the reason why Yeats, at this time, had difficulty in identifying the quarter from which he was being attacked was that it was too painful for him to identify his new enemy: Catholic nationalism. Yeats had been a nationalist, politically as well as culturally, since 1887. He was as he said "an Irish nationalist of the school of John O'Leary", and it was at O'Leary's house that he had met Maud Gonne. O'Leary had told him that "in Ireland a man must have either the Church or the Fenians on his side and you will never have the Church". Yeats had taken that advice to heart and cultivated an ultra-nationalist image. The turn of the century, from 1898 to 1902, was the period of Yeats's greatest nationalist activity. In 1898, he had taken a prominent part, along with Maud Gonne, in the centenary commemoration of the Rising of 1898. In 1900 he had taken a prominent part, also along with Maud Gonne, in the demonstrations against Queen Victoria's visit to Ireland. Both these positions were more advanced, in nationalist terms, than the mainstream nationalism of the day, and they were also strongly disapproved of by all unionists, that is to say by most Protestants.

Rejected by Protestant unionists, for reasons of his own choice, he now – for reasons which seem to have taken him altogether by surprise – found that the radical nationalists of Irish Ireland were being urged to reject him as a West Briton. He was in danger of breaking O'Leary's Law, and having both the Church and the Fenians against him.

Technically, *The Leader* was not a Fenian organ, but represented a Church-approved cultural-nationalist ginger-group within constitutional nationalism (but approved also by some Republicans). But such fine distinctions had to be unstable in the context of nationalism, which is much more a complex of emotions than a body of doctrine. The Irish-Irelanders of 1900 to 1914 were to provide the Irish Republicans of 1916. Patrick Pearse, in the days before he became a revolutionary, was a declared adherent to Irish Ireland, and not merely a reader of *The Leader* but an advertiser in it. There were other Irish-Ireland periodicals besides *The Leader* – Arthur Griffith's *Sinn Féin* for example – but *The Leader* was by far the most lively organ in this category, the best supported by advertisers and probably the most widely-read. The booksellers were registering the severe impact of Moran's attacks, by the summer of 1901.

In the following months and years, *The Leader* developed its specific campaign against Yeats and the Irish Literary Movement, within its general crusade for Faith and Fatherland. In its issue of 27 July, 1901, *The Leader* carried an article, "Protestants and the Irish Nation", which both puts Protestant aspirants to nationalist status in their place ideologically and doctrinally, and then goes on to take a personal (but deniable) swipe at Yeats himself. In the doctrinal bit *The Leader* defines the role of "non-Catholics" in relation to Irish Ireland.

"The few non-Catholics who would like to throw in their lot with the Irish nation must recognise that the Irish nation is *de facto* a Catholic nation, just as the English Catholic recognises that England is a Protestant nation. We desire to realise an Irish Ireland and let the non-Catholics help in the work or get out of the system. Their kin have robbed us and enslaved us and interrupted our development as a nation. They owe us restitution."

The personal swipe runs as follows:

"He [not named] sometimes writes poetry which no Irishman understands, or rather which no Irishman troubles his head to read; he thinks Catholics are superstitious and he believes in spooks himself; he thinks they are priest-ridden and he would like to go back to Paganism; he is a bigot who thinks he is broadminded; a prig who thinks he is cultured; he does not understand Ireland."

Moran here seems to realise that he is going too far in personal abuse, for he adds, as if taking a deep breath:

"However, he means well, and he might be left to time and experience for the acquirement of sense, only that he has no small distractive power, in this unthinking and cringing land. Of course this description does not apply to any individual."

The perfidious disclaimer is uncharacteristic. Normally, candour is the characteristic that distinguishes Moran from other Catholic nationalists, at this time and since. One feels that something in Moran, at this point, is ashamed of what he was doing. If so, Moran soon recovered and resumed the attack. Late in 1901 a new play was put on in Yeats's theatre. This was *Diarmuid and Grainne* by George Moore and WB Yeats. *The Leader* reviewed the play by these two Irish Protestant writers, under the rubric: "The English Mind in Ireland". Their reviewer wrote: "They have offered an insult to our mind and heart, by their misrepresentation of the story in its moral aspect. The character of Grainne has been gratuitously defiled by the hand of the English mind. From the beginning of the Fenian story to the end there is not one line that could be twisted into a suggestion of unfaithfulness on her part." This gloss on the medieval saga depends on a casuistical interpretation of pagan marriage-customs: Grainne seduces Diarmuid into fleeing with her from the marriage-feast only, not from the marriage-bed . . .The reviewer then goes on to describe the Yeats-Moore Grainne as "the vile woman of this coarse English play". The reviewer concluded: "Let the English mind in future write plays for itself. We will have none of them" (*The Leader*, 2 November, 1901).

Oddly enough, the same issue carried an article by Lady Gregory whose mind, one would suppose, was no less, and no more English than those of WB Yeats and George Moore.[23] But inconsequence and hyperbole are part of the culture.

The attack on *Diarmuid and Grainne*, like the play itself, seems to have fallen rather flat. Yet *The Leader* review is of interest for two reasons, in the general history of the relationship between Irish Ireland (Catholics) and the Irish Literary Movement (Protestants). The review takes up the theme of intruding alien unchastity, hitherto directed against the commercial theatre in Dublin, and turns it against Yeats's theatre, seen as allied with the British commercial theatre, in the English mind's attempt to debauch the pure Irish mind. The review looks back to the earlier attacks on the commercial theatre. But it also looks forward to a possible theme in future attacks on Yeats's theatre. *The Leader* would be vigilant, henceforward, for any signs of sexual impurity in that Protestant-run theatre. Such opportunities did not often present themselves: *Zasa*-type shows were not part of the

---

23. The fact of Lady Gregory's contributions eased my mind a little concerning my father's contributions.

Abbey repertoire. When an opportunity did present itself, with *The Playboy of the Western World*, the Catholic-nationalist puritans of Irish Ireland took it with both hands. *The Playboy* riots cannot be properly understood except against the background of *The Leader*'s sustained political-sectarian campaign against what Yeats represented.

At the time of *Diarmuid and Grainne*, however, *The Playboy* was six years in the future. I have now to consider the play that Yeats wrote and staged in the year following *Diarmuid and Grainne*: a play that is of prime importance in the history of nationalism in Ireland.

CATHLEEN NI HOULIHAN (1902)

Cathleen ni Houlihan is both the most nationalist and the most propagandist work that Yeats ever wrote. It is probably the most powerful piece of nationalist propaganda that has ever been composed. It has certainly never been excelled in that domain by anything that has been composed and presented, before or since, in Ireland.

WB Yeats's father, the liberal painter, John B Yeats, wrote to WB: "You have been liable at times, only at times, to a touch of the propaganda fiend" (December, 1913). Usually, it was no more than a touch.[24] But in the case of *Cathleen ni Houlihan*, the writer is in the grip of the fiend in question from the beginning to the end of the short electrifying play.

As is universally acknowledged, the genesis of any work of art is a mysterious matter. But when a work of art is also a work of propaganda, the motivation of its author need not be beyond all conjecture. In the two years before the composition of *Cathleen*, Yeats had been taunted, not only with not being a nationalist, but with not being *capable* of being a nationalist. It does not seem far-fetched in this context

---

24. For Yeats's politics in general, see my essay "Passion and Cunning: An Essay on the Politics of WB Yeats," in *Passion and Cunning: Essays on Nationalism, Terror and Revolution* (New York and London, 1988). The only other work of Yeats that can compare with *Cathleen ni Houlihan*, in intensity of nationalist propaganda, is the late poem "The Ghost of Roger Casement" (1938)

to entertain the idea that Yeats wrote this play to show his nationalist detractors that he was a more effective nationalist writer than any of the rest of them had it in them to be. And *Cathleen ni Houlihan* did establish just that. He was also concerned to please Maud Gonne, a fierce nationalist; the two motives converged.

We know from the same letter to Lady Gregory from which I have already quoted, that Yeats was not personally in a particularly nationalistic mood in the period immediately preceding the composition of *Cathleen ni Houlihan*. We know that he was also worried at the decline in popular support for him in Ireland: a decline which was due to the Catholic-nationalist campaign against him, though Yeats never seems to have referred explicitly to that ominous combination. In that letter to Lady Gregory, Yeats says: "I imagine that, as I withdraw from politics my friends among the nationalists will grow less, at first at any rate, and my foes more numerous. What I hear from Bullen only confirms the idea that I had at the time of the *Countess Cathleen* row that it would make a very serious difference in my position outside the small cultured class".

"It." Yeats is here obliquely, and perhaps unconsciously acknowledging the fusion of Catholicism and nationalism in the campaign against his theatre, and he knew that "it" was damaging "my position outside the small cultured class". And he was still, in 1901-2, concerned with defending that position. In a letter to Lady Gregory, written immediately after the successful production of *Cathleen ni Houlihan* Yeats wrote: "I have a plan for a little religious play in one act with quite as striking a plot as *Cathleen* – it cannot offend anybody and may propitiate Holy Church".[25]

The "little religious play" does not seem to have been written, at least in this period, but Yeats went out of the propitiation business shortly after he wrote that letter. The idea may possibly have been reworked later and turned into *Calvary* (1920). I don't know that Holy Church was impressed.

25. Yeats to Lady Gregory, 10 April, 1902; A Wade, *Letters of W.B. Yeats* p. 370

It looks very much as if Yeats, in that spring of 1902, was hoping for a kind of double: the propitiation of Irish nationalism and Irish Catholicism. He did not succeed, on either front, and it is just as well for his art that he did not.

Yet *Cathleen ni Houlihan* was a great success at the time, and had a powerful influence on the development of Irish nationalism in the following fourteen years. But before looking at the influence, let us take a brief look at the play itself.

Cathleen (aka Kathleen) ni Houlihan is a mythical being, the best known of a number of female names used to personify Ireland in Gaelic poetry. Yeats's play of that name is set in Killala, Co Mayo, in 1798, at the time of the landing of a French Revolutionary force. Cathleen takes the form of a Poor Old Woman; in Irish *Sean Bhean Bhocht*, another name for the female incarnation of Ireland. The Poor Old Woman visits – and it is indeed a visitation – the home of a fairly prosperous Catholic farming family, the Gillanes, who are preparing for the marriage of the young Michael Gillane. The Old Woman is there to cancel the marriage, and replace it with a blood-sacrifice, in a nationalist revolution. Bridget, Michael's mother, begins by assuming that the Old Woman is no more than what she seems to be:

"Bridget: It is a wonder that you are not worn out with so much wandering.

"Old Woman: Sometimes my feet are tired and my hands are quiet, but there is no quiet in my heart. When the people see me quiet, they think old age has come on me and that all the stir has gone out of me [*a reference to the apparent disappearance of revolutionary nationalism in the Ireland of the early twentieth century*]. But when the trouble is on me I must be talking to my friends [*the revolutionary nationalists*].[26]

"Bridget: What was it put you wandering?

"Old Woman: Too many strangers in the house [*the British*].

"Bridget: Indeed you look as if you'd had your share of trouble.

---

26. These references would have been absolutely obvious to a Dublin audience in 1902, as they are also to Irish nationalists today. But I cannot assume that they are equally so to all my readers, including those who are outside Ireland.

> "*Old Woman:* I have had trouble indeed.
> "*Bridget:* What was it put the trouble on you?
> "*Old Woman:* My four beautiful green fields."

The four beautiful green fields are the Four Provinces of Ireland. The fact that a part of the Fourth Green Field – Ulster – is withheld from Cathleen ni Houlihan by the strangers in her house motivates and validates the armed struggle of the Provisional IRA today. Moderate nationalists repudiate the armed struggle, but accept the validity of its objective: restoring the integrity of the Four Green Fields. This gives the IRA an inbuilt moral advantage over the moderate nationalists: again, that differential is at work.

In the play, Peter Gillane, Michael's father, offers the Poor Old Woman a shilling and she refuses.

> "*Peter:* What is it you would be asking for?
> "*Old Woman:* If any one would give me help he must give me himself, he must give me all.

The Old Woman makes clear that death is what she is about:

> "*Old Woman* [who is standing in the doorway]: They are wondering that there were songs made for me; there have been many songs for me. I heard one in the wind this morning:
> [Sings]
> *Do not make a great keening*
> *When the graves have been dug tomorrow.*
> *Do not call the white-scarfed riders*
> *To the burying that shall be tomorrow*
> *Do not spread food to call strangers*
> *To the wakes that shall be tomorrow;*
> *Do not give money for prayers*
> *For the dead that shall die tomorrow . . .*
> *They will have no need of prayers,*
> *They will have no need of prayers.*

That last repeated assertion is of great interest with regard to the relationship between nationalism and Catholicism. Cathleen is a quasi-divine being, felt to be anterior to Catholicism, not bound by its laws, but capable of dispensing from their application; as in this instance. Yeats is addressing himself to those Catholic nationalists in whom nationalism, in any conflict with Catholicism, has to prevail. This phenomenon is not confined to Ireland. The great French Catholic nationalist Charles Péguy (1873-1914) explicitly exempts things done in the name of French nationalism from the jurisdiction of God. In *Le Mystère de la Charité de Jeanne d'Arc* (1910) Peguy affirms that God could not condemn Joan of Arc. And he adds: "And even if God wanted to do that, it's no business of his"

Et quand Dieu le voudrait, ce n'est pas son affaire.

In Ireland, at this time, people of this stamp were called Fenians (aka, Republicans). Mindful of the advice of John O'Leary, Yeats, through Cathleen ni Houlihan, is addressing the Fenians and the young admirers of the Fenians. He is implicitly appealing from the Moran version of Irish nationalism to a higher nationalist jurisdiction. *The Leader* people were constitutional nationalists, of a relatively advanced variety, and they also regularly flaunted their Catholic orthodoxy. In asserting that the Fenian dead have no need of prayers, because they died for Ireland, Yeats is asserting the primacy of Irish nationalism over Irish Catholicism. He is also, nostalgically and subliminally, touching the string of an almost-forgotten Parnellism, reminding his audiences of the time, less than ten years before, when nationalist Dublin never challenged the credentials of a Protestant Parnellite. Yeats's political insights and controversial skills are often underestimated.

In the play, Cathleen's concluding speech sets out the conditions of her service, and how the service will be rewarded.

Old Woman: It is a hard service they take that help me. Many that are red-cheeked now will be pale-cheeked; many that have been free to walk the hills and the bogs and the rushes will be sent to walk hard streets in far countries; many that have gathered money will not stay to spend it; many a child will be born and there will be no father at its christening to give it a name. They that have red cheeks will have pale cheeks for my sake, and for all that, they will think that they are well paid. [*She goes out; her voice is heard outside singing*]

> *They shall be remembered for ever,*
> *They shall be alive for ever,*
> *They shall be speaking for ever,*
> *The people shall hear them for ever.*

The end of the play runs as follows:

Patrick [a lad of twelve, Michael's brother]: There are ships in the Bay: the French are landing at Killala.

[*Peter takes his pipe from his mouth and his hat off and stands up* – [saluting the advent of the sacral]. *The* [wedding] *clothes slip from Michael's arm.*

Delia [Michael's fiancée] Michael! [*He takes no notice*] Michael! [*He turns towards her*] Why do you look at me like a stranger? [*She drops his arm. Bridget goes over towards her.*]

Patrick: The boys are all hurrying down the hillside to join the French.

Delia: Michael won't be going to join the French.

Bridget [to Peter]: Tell him not to go, Peter.

Peter: It's no use. He doesn't hear a word we're saying.

Bridget: Try and coax him over to the fire.

Delia: Michael! Michael! You won't leave me! You won't join the French and we going to be married! [*She puts her arms about him, he turns towards her as if about to yield*]

Old Woman's voice outside:

They shall be speaking for ever,

The people shall hear them for ever.

[*Michael breaks away from Delia, stands for a second at the door, then rushes out, following the Old Woman's voice.*

Bridget takes Delia, who is crying silently, in her arms].

The first sentence of the above stage direction was of critical importance to the success of the play. It was not in the play as originally written by Yeats, who would have left Michael hesitating between Delia and the call of the Old Woman. The change was made during rehearsal at the request, or behest, of Maud Gonne, always a stronger nationalist than Yeats (that differential again). Maud Gonne who was rehearsing her part as Cathleen, wrote to Yeats:

"We rehearsed Kathleen tonight, it went splendidly, all but the end. It doesn't make a good curtain. We are all of opinion [presumably the cast, but perhaps some Republican friends also] that Michael ought to go right out of the door instead of standing hesitating. It doesn't seem clear if he doesn't go out. If he goes out Delia can throw herself on Bridget's shoulder in tears which makes a much better end."[27]

The play ends: *Peter*. [*to Patrick, laying a hand on his arm*]. Did you see an old woman going down the path?

Patrick: I did not, but I saw a young girl, and she had the walk of a queen.

Irish nationalists of the fiercer sort have always found that *dénouement* eminently satisfactory, edifying in its priorities - the dumping of a living woman at the call of a personified Nation — and a standing inspiration to the Republican Movement. Nationalists of milder descriptions (who are of course far more numerous) tend to find the scene, and the play, artistically and historically impressive, no doubt, but faintly embarrassing and in any case no longer relevant to contemporary conditions. The fiercer nationalists, however, have their ways of demonstrating the contemporary relevance of their message and mandate from Cathleen ni Houlihan.

The milder or constitutional nationalists, over the past twenty-five years, have seemed paralysed, and as if mesmerised, by the lethal assurance of those who, like

27. Letter dated Monday Night [March 1902] in Anna MacBride White and A Norman Jeffares (eds) *The Gonne-Yeats Letters 1893 – 1938* (New York and London, 1992-3) p. 150

Michael Gillane in his time, respond to Cathleen's summons in our own day. The constitutional nationalists look like Peter Gillane as he "takes his pipe from his mouth and his hat off and stands up". They're a respectful and inert lot, our constitutional nationalists of today, in the presence of a stronger nationalism than their own. This is the differential that may yet destroy us.

Cathleen ni Houlihan was put on at St Teresa's Hall, Clarendon Street, Dublin on 2, 3 and 4 April, 1902. Maud Gonne, of course, played the Old Woman. The play aroused great enthusiasm among young and passionate nationalists, especially Republicans, but serious misgivings among older constitutional ones. Stephen Gwynn, one of the latter, wrote: "The effect of Cathleen ni Houlihan on me was that I went home asking myself if such plays should be produced unless one was prepared for people to go out to shoot and be shot . . . Miss Gonne's impersonation had stirred the audience as I have never seen another audience stirred".[28]

Significantly, revolutionary members of the audience, recalling the impression the play made on them, used religious terminology. PS O'Hegarty stated long afterwards that to him *Cathleen ni Houlihan* was "a sort of sacrament".[29] Constance Markievicz, when under sentence of death for her part in the 1916 Rising wrote: "That play of WB's was a sort of gospel to me".[30]

There is, of course, nothing overtly religious in the play. On the contrary – or apparently to the contrary – prayers are mentioned, only to be dismissed. Yet the central idea is basically a religious one, and this must have been felt by the audience. The central idea is *vocation.* Michael hears the Call and rejects his terrestrial bride-to-be:

"*Old Woman:* It is not a man going to his marriage that I look to for help . . . *Michael breaks away from Delia.*"

28. Quoted in AN Jeffares, *W.B. Yeats*, p. 138
29. O'Hegarty, "W.B. Yeats and the Revolutionary Ireland of his time" *Dublin Magazine*, July-September, 1939
30. Constance was writing to her sister Eva Gore-Booth, from Aylesbury Prison.

The nationalist revolutionary élite is felt to be a sacral order, on the same footing as the Catholic priesthood and equally above question. Cathleen ni Houlihan was a divinity, and the Call from her was as valid as the Call from Jesus Christ. Yeats was not a Catholic, but he knew his Catholic audience, and aided by Maud Gonne had an instinct for what would have power over it.

Yeats did not of course invent Cathleen ni Houlihan. She had been around for centuries, in poems and stories. But Yeats brought Cathleen to life – or a kind of death-in-life – on the stage. He brought her into conjunction with the proto-revolutionary politics of the early twentieth century. And above all, he endowed her with unforgettable words and an irresistible promise.

"They shall be remembered forever" quoted Constance Markievicz in her death-cell in Aylesbury Prison and she added "and even poor me shall not be forgotten". Yeats, on his death-bed, thirty-seven years later, asked:

Did that play of mine send out
Certain men the English shot?

On the evidence of the witnesses I have cited, (and others we shall consider) we can safely assume that it did. But then Yeats had been addressing himself to people whom he knew already to be wanting to hear a sacral summons brought out of the national past. He brought them the message they yearned for.

The overwhelming success of *Cathleen ni Houlihan,* on the nationalist front, temporarily silenced Yeats's Catholic-nationalist enemies in Ireland. In other circumstances, Cathleen's dismissal of prayers for the dead might have offered a tempting target for *The Leader.* as expressive of Protestant contempt for Catholic practices. But DP Moran was too wily a bird to try that one, in the circumstances of April, 1902. He knew his nationalist readers were crazy about *Cathleen.* He would bide his time. And the Church itself – so vigilant about heresy in *Countess Cathleen* – gave no sign of concern about Cathleen's dismissal of prayers for the dead who died for Ireland. *Countess Cathleen* had not been a nationalist play. *Cathleen ni Houlihan* was, and an alarmingly successful one at that. Best to observe a prudent silence. The Church does not lightly risk confrontation with aroused nationalism.

Did churchmen sense, in the success of *Cathleen ni Houlihan,* a manifestation of a rival religion? Some of them, surely, must have known that there were Catholic nationalists who felt *Cathleen ni Houlihan* to be a sort of "sacrament" or "gospel". But I don't think experienced Irish priests would worry much about that. "Sort of", best to treat it as a metaphor, really, not a rival religion, but an aspect of life in Catholic and nationalist Ireland: some of the religious feelings naturally overflow into the politics. That's the way it is, and you can't change it, just treat it with the utmost circumspection. Pity, though, that Yeats is messing around with sensitive matters that are no business of the likes of him. Have to keep an eye on that fellow.

The Leader reviewed *Cathleen ni Houlihan* briefly and condescendingly on 11 April, 1902. "Mr Yeats", said the reviewer, "is beginning to see the light." This implied that Yeats had learned to write his nationalist play by studying the columns of *The Leader*. The reality was very different. *The Leader's* nationalism, though truculently expressed, and accompanied by unusually open sectarianism, was basically mild enough politically speaking: constitutional nationalism, aggressively expressed. *Cathleen ni Houlihan* was the real stuff: revolutionary propaganda, outright Republicanism. Inwardly, DP Moran must have been shaken. Yeats was becoming a bigger force in Nationalist Ireland than Moran had ever bargained for. The Catholic-nationalist effort to freeze him out seemed to have failed.

YEATS AND MAUD GONNE DIVERGE

Yet Moran had really no need to worry. Yeats, as we have seen, even while incubating *Cathleen ni Houlihan,* was wearying of politics and specifically of nationalist politics. An event in his personal life, less than a year after the first production of that play, completed his disenchantment and estranged him from the nationalist cause, as that cause was understood by the play's audiences. At some time in January 1903, Maud Gonne broke it to Yeats that she was about to become a Catholic and marry Major John MacBride, a hero to nationalist Ireland because he had fought against the British in the Boer War (1899-1902). After the blow had fallen, Yeats wrote a long and agonised, and in parts incoherent, letter to Maud Gonne. The letter is of interest to us in the context of our present study because it reveals how strong feelings about religion and nationalism can be intertwined with strong feelings about caste and class, and strong personal feelings. Major John MacBride, unlike Yeats and Maud Gonne, belonged, for Yeats, to what were then called "the lower orders" – most Irish Catholics did. Yeats wrote (in part):

". . . If you carry out your purpose you will fall into a lower order to do great injury to the religeon [sic: WBY's spelling was always weak] of free souls that is growing up in Ireland, it may be to enlighten the whole world. A man said to me last night having seen the announcement in the papers 'The priests will all triumph, exult over us all for generations because of this.' You possess your influence in Ireland very largely because you came to the people from above. You represent a superior class, a class whose people are more independent, have a more beautiful life, a more refined life. But Maud Gonne is about to pass away . . . you are going to marry one of the people." At this point in the letter, Yeats gets somewhat out of control. The text in *The Gonne-Yeats Letters* goes on: "This [?] weakness which has <has> [thrust] down your soul to a lower order of faith is thrusting you down socially is thrusting you down to the people, you will have no longer any thing to give only those who are above them can [indecipherable] you to [?] rob and then of robbing you. They will never forgive it – This [?they] [are] the most aristocratic-minded [people] the most thirsting for what is above them

71

and beyond them, of living people . . . "

At the end of this letter, Yeats tries to influence Maud Gonne with a classic statement of anti-clerical nationalism, school of John O'Leary:

"Is it the priest, when the day of great hazard has come who will lead the people. No, no. He will palter with the government is [as?] he did at the Act of Union, as he did when he denounced the Fenians. He will say 'Be quiet, be good cristians [sic] do not shed blood'. It is [?is it] not the priest who has [?softened] the will of our young men – who has broken their pride. You have said all these things not so long ago. For [it] is not only the trust of your friends but your own soul that you are about to betray."[31]

On 10 February, 1903 Maud Gonne replied to Yeats, from the Convent in Laval where she was being prepared for her Catholic baptism. The passages that concern us here take up Yeats's points about religion and nationality. Naturally, she takes the opposing point of view to Yeats: she holds now that the two go together. She has joined the ranks of the Catholic nationalists. Maud Gonne writes:

"About my change of Religion I believe like you that there is one great universal truth. God that pervades everything. I believe that each religion is a different prism through which one looks at truth . . . Our nation looks at God through one prism, The Catholic Religion [MG's initial capitals]. I am officially a protestant [MG's lower case initial] supposed to look at it from another, a much narrower one which is moreover the English one. I prefer to look at truth through the same prism as my country people – I am going to become a Catholic. It seems to be of small importance if one calls the great spirit forces the *Sidhe*, the Gods [?or] the Archangels for the great symbols of all religions are the same – But I do feel it important *not* to belong to the Church of England."[32]

No good Irish nationalist could contest that last one.

Later that month, after her baptism, Maud Gonne wrote

31. Anna MacBride and A Norman Jeffares [eds], *The Gonne-Yeats Letters 1893-1938*, pp. 164-6
32. *Gonne-Yeats Letters*, pp. 166-7

again to Yeats. She was anxious to let him know, as from one Irish nationalist to another, the manner in which she had complied with the ecclesiastical requirement that the person to be baptised must abjure heresy. She wrote:

". . . I hated having to abjure anything – I refused completely to do so in the form presented to me. In it I was required to declare hatred of all heresies. I said I hated nothing in the world but the British Empire which I looked on as the outward symbol of Satan in the world where ever it came in [in the course of the ceremony] I was to declare hatred of heresy. I declared hatred of the British Empire, on this form I made my solemn abjuration of Anglicism, declaration of hatred of England.[33]

The baptism was performed by Monsignor Pierre-Joseph Geay, Bishop of Laval.[34] The Bishop made no objection to Maud Gonne's theological formula. No doubt he was a good French nationalist. Renouncing an English heresy was good, but a declaration of hatred of England was an even more acceptable proof of Catholicism.

After Maud Gonne's baptism and marriage, Yeats did not give up on nationalism: at least he did not think of himself as doing so. Late in life he said: "All my life I have been an Irish nationalist of the school of John O'Leary". What he did give up was nationalist propaganda; his theatre would not be a vehicle for nationalist propaganda: *Cathleen ni Houlihan* would be the last effort in that line of his activity.[35]

Propaganda is necessarily a populist enterprise and after Major John MacBride had devastated his life, Yeats had had his fill of populism. As he later wrote:

---

33. Gonne to Yeats, 24 February [1905]: *Gonne-Yeats Letters*, pp 167-8. Maud Gonne was English, and the daughter of an English army officer. English converts to Irish nationalism often feel the need to be particularly fervent in declarations of hatred against England

34. *Gonne-Yeats Letters*, p. 491, n. 124

35. He turned again to nationalist propaganda at the very end of his life, with the ballad "The Ghost of Roger Casement" (1938). His 1916 poems (published in 1920) are not propaganda, though they can be quoted for propaganda purposes. See *Passion and Cunning*.

My love is angry that of late
I cry all base blood down
As though she had not taught me hate
By kisses to a clown.

The change in Yeats was not immediately apparent, even to Maud Gonne. In May of 1903, just after her marriage to MacBride, she wrote two eager letters inviting his participation in – and assuming his sympathy for – a new People's Protection Committee whose object was to make as much trouble as possible on the occasion of the coming visit to Ireland of King Edward VII. Yeats had assisted a similar effort on the occasion of the last Royal visit – Queen Victoria's in 1900 – and Maud Gonne writes as if nothing had changed. She seems to have assumed that their clash over religion left them still allies over nationalism. But this was not a safe assumption, either in Irish conditions generally, or in this particular case. Yeats did not come aboard for the People's Protection Committee, but Maud Gonne went ahead, with the support of the kind of people who had most passionately applauded her in *Cathleen ni Houlihan* the year before. The editors of the Gonne-Yeats letters write:

"Maud Gonne had her own private demonstration. The Pope had died and in protest against the unionist bunting decorating the unionist houses in her quiet cul-de-sac she hung a black flag of mourning out of her window, the flag being a black petticoat on a broom handle. Police arrived to remove it, loyalists gathered and sang 'God Save the King', nationalists came and sang, 'A Nation Once Again'. The police cordoned off Coulson Avenue, but Maud Gonne was protected by a group of young hurlers with their sticks."[36]

One wonders how this marvellous lady managed to get around, while her habitual mode of conveyance was tied up in this way?

Maud Gonne's black petticoat – simultaneously mourning

---

36. *Gonne-Yeats Letters*, p. 172

for the Pope and spurning the King of England – was her own way of asserting her combined loyalty to Catholicism and Irish nationalism (although it was not a way of which most Catholic nationalists would have approved at the time). But Yeats – who was no longer to be drawn into undignified Gonne-style shenanigans – had his own way of protesting against this Royal visit, and his way, unlike Maud's, put nationalism and Catholicism into conflict, in the old Fenian tradition. In August, the Fenian periodical the *United Irishman* carried a sarcastic letter from WB Yeats about Edward VII's visit to Maynooth. *The Times* (London) had carried a report about the room in the College prepared for the reception of the King-Emperor: "the walls were draped in His Majesty's racing colours and carried two admirable engravings of royal horses Ambush 11 and Diamond Jubilee."[37]

Yeats commented: "Even a heretic like myself can admire the loyalty, so perfect that it becomes an enthusiasm, not only for the King in his public capacity, but for his private tastes. I expect to read in the sporting column of *The Irish Times* that Cardinal Logue has something on Sceptre and that Archbishop Walsh has a little bit of all right for the Chester Cup".

Yeats's letter may have pleased and amused some readers of the *United Irishman*, but it would have annoyed most Irish nationalists who came to know of it at the time. Most nationalists were Home Rulers, not separatists, and not Republicans. The person whom the Republicans always called "the King of England" would be "King of Great Britain and Ireland" in a Home Rule settlement. The Irish Parliamentary Party were ready to settle for that, and so were the Catholic Hierarchy. Those who organised the Royal reception at Maynooth thought of themselves as good nationalists, and that their reception would make Home Rule more acceptable. This was the year of the Wyndham Act (enabling tenant farmers to buy their land, on advantageous conditions) and Anglo-Irish

---

37. *The Letters of W.B. Yeats* (ed Wade) p. 408; the *United Irishman* published the letter on 1 August, 1903.

relations were overall unusually good. Even the sort of "advanced" Catholic constitutional nationalists, represented by Irish Ireland and *The Leader*, did not support protests against the visit. There was, as usual a good deal of ambivalence around, but most Catholics and most nationalists would have resented a sneer at the Cardinal and the Archbishops coming from a self-styled "heretic" – and perhaps resented it all the more when the sneer was purportedly directed from an extreme nationalist position (and with a trace of social condescension).

Maud Gonne certainly could not be mollified by Yeats's protest against the Royal visit, given the idiosyncratic and apparently anti-Catholic form it had assumed. By September, Maud Gonne had taken note that Yeats's theatre was no longer a temple of Cathleen ni Houlihan. She wrote to Yeats: "I still think it would be best for me to cease to be the vice-president of the Theatre Co., I won't undertake any but National fights, the theatre Co does not seem inclined for such 'fights'".[38]

Shortly afterwards, Maud Gonne formally resigned from the Theatre. She added: "I am sorry to write all this which I know will be distasteful to you but with me *the National idea is a religion,* [my italics CCO'B] a Theatre Co unless it serves the National cause seems to me of little importance."[39]

Yeats's theatre was now being regarded with growing suspicion by nationalists generally, in addition to those avowedly Catholic-nationalist circles which had suspected it all along.

In October, 1903, *The Leader* carried an article, out of the blue as it were, entitled: "The Philosophy of an Irish Theatre" of which the following is the core: "The Irish people are Christian, they believe in the morality of the Catholic Church, and they will not suffer any attempt to pervert their opinions on such matters, or to misrepresent their attitudes towards such problems": (31 October, 1903).

The article (unusually) has no peg, but I believe it to be

---

38. *Gonne-Yeats Letters,* p. 173
39. *Gonne-Yeats Letters,* p. 178

responsive to Yeats's August letter to *United Ireland* in which he speaks in the persona of "a heretic", who is also a strong nationalist.

As the decade wore on, Yeats's friends came to be exclusively drawn from the "small cultivated class" of which he had spoken and his theatre was increasingly attracting unionists and West Britons. *The Leader* noted this development in an article "At the Abbey Theatre" (7 Jan. 1905): "With our eyes fixed on the stalls, we might have thought, were it not that John Redmond was in our line of vision, that we had strayed into some prayer-meeting of the foreign element in Ireland."

That was the stalls, but there were Irish Irelanders in the pit; an explosive mixture, as the future was to show.

Commenting on the West Britons in the stalls, *The Leader* sneers: "*Kathleen ni Houlihan* makes Irish patriotism quite harmless, if not respectable."

This comment suggests that by now (early 1905) *The Leader* is getting out of touch with the section of its own Irish-Ireland constituency that would be most important for the future: young nationalists with revolutionary yearnings. For these, as we have seen *Cathleen ni Houlihan* could be "a sort of sacrament" or "a sort of gospel". Yeats had given up on nationalist propaganda but the masterpiece in that genre which he had created was still keeping the flame alive, ready to flare up, in appropriate conditions. In that respect Yeats in this period can be compared to Frankenstein, watching his monster get out of control.

That *Leader* article concluded on an Olympian note: "Mr Yeats does not interest us". Nothing could be further from the truth.

THE FALL AND RESURRECTION OF MAUD GONNE

The Leader had been out to get Yeats and his theatre, as we have seen, since its foundation at the beginning of the century. It was still out to get him, and it knew he was now much more vulnerable. In 1902, newly girt with an armour of sacral nationalism, as the author of *Cathleen ni Houlihan*, recently performed by Maud Gonne with staggering success, Yeats had seemed invulnerable. By the middle of the decade, that magic had faded. Maud Gonne had resigned from Yeats's theatre, on nationalist grounds in 1903. And then Maud Gonne herself had fallen, by 1905-6, into comprehensive disgrace, with all shadings of Catholics and nationalists, as a result of the separation and divorce proceedings instituted by her in Paris against Major John MacBride.

The evidence, which was quite grisly, showed beyond doubt that MacBride was the guilty party. But hardly anyone in Catholic and nationalist Ireland gave a damn about the evidence. What mattered was the nationalist and Catholic status of the contending parties. Major John MacBride was not only a nationalist hero but *the* nationalist hero of the early twentieth century. Irish nationalists were strongly pro-Boer, but felt a bit guilty that the Boers were fighting the British, and the Irish actually weren't at the time. By joining the Boers and fighting the British, MacBride was felt to have removed that stigma, and redeemed the honour of the Irish race. No finer fellow ever breathed than Major John MacBride, was the feeling among nationalists at the time. And so any charges levelled against Major MacBride, particularly charges of sexual misbehaviour, were automatically false, vile calumnies, no doubt instigated by the British.

This disposition of Catholic and nationalist minds comprehensively damned Maud Gonne. From a nationalist point of view, she was calumniating an Irish hero, presumably at British instigation. From a Catholic point of view, her attempt to secure a divorce – forbidden to Catholics – proved that her conversion to Catholicism had been a fake. Maud Gonne told Yeats, in a letter written from Paris, towards the end of 1905, of the picture of her presented during the judicial proceedings by Mâitre Labori, MacBride's counsel: "[Labori said] that I am an English woman – that I only became Catholic to marry MacBride and have now become Protestant to divorce."[40]

---

40. *Gonne-Yeats Letters*, p. 220. Maitre Labori was a hero of the Left in the Paris of the day; he had defended Zola in the Dreyfus Case. In Paris, Maud Gonne's political friends were on the Right. She had been the mistress of the prominent Right-wing politician, Lucien Millevoye, by whom she had a daughter Iseult, to whom Yeats later proposed. Iseult married the novelist, Francis Stuart

Of the three charges, it seems that the one that Maud Gonne felt to be by far the most damaging was "English woman". She was anxious, at this time, to circulate family papers showing that ancestors of hers had come to Ireland from Caithness in Scotland in the late sixteenth century. I don't know if she did ever circulate such documents, but if she did they will have done her no good at all. Maud Gonne's sense of Irish history was emotionally strong but intellectually approximate. To any *born* Irish nationalist, that record would suggest, not that her ancestors were Irish, but that they were among the invaders and robbers and oppressors of the Irish people against whom Maud Gonne was directing so much stirring oratory throughout her life.

So from any possible Irish Catholic or nationalist point of view Maud Gonne was the pits, circa 1906. No one who knew how she stood then could imagine that she could ever stage a comeback as a nationalist heroine. Yet she did – and "stage" is the word – ten years later, in 1916. When the husband whom she loathed was shot by a British firing-squad, after the Easter Rising, Madame MacBride – as she now came to be known – attired herself from head to toe in the most spectacular set of widow's weeds ever seen in Dublin, to which she returned from Paris in 1917. Her mourning for Major John MacBride was so intense that it lasted all the remaining years of her life (nearly forty of them), as far as outward appearances were concerned. I still remember her as I first saw her in that garb, about ten years later in Leinster Road, Rathmines. With her great height and noble carriage, her pale beaked gaunt face, and large lustrous eyes, and gliding along in that great flapping cloud of black, she seemed like the Angel of Death: or more precisely, like the crow-like bird, the Morrigu, that heralds Death in the Gaelic sagas. That is how I think of that vision in retrospect; at the time I just thought: "spooky"!

Meeting her later, at her home, Roebuck House, Clonskeagh, Dublin, where my Aunt Hanna brought me from time to time, I found her less impressive. Especially when she

79

talked. But as a spectacle – in the street, on a platform or the stage – she was incomparable.

"Madame" – as she became known exclusively, after the death of the other "Madame," Countess Markievicz and Madame O'Rahilly (widow of The O'Rahilly) – became the principal symbolic figure in a new and potent group in Irish politics: the Widows of 1916, the new guardian-Priestesses of the nationalist faith. Everyone knew of course that, whereas the other widows were in genuine (though far less conspicuous and sustained) mourning for their martyred husbands, Madame couldn't possibly feel any personal grief for the individual whose name she bore, and whose weeds she wore. The details of the ghastly contention between the Major and Maud in 1905-6 were long forgotten by 1916, but people knew, in a general way, that the two had been hopelessly estranged. (She was said, in the folk-version, to have accused him of "coming to bed in his boots"). But this, far from detracting from the merit of her mourning, was felt to enhance its dignity. The other widows had personal cause to mourn. Her mourning, alone, was pure, abstract, gratuitous *national* mourning and the grandiose hieratic character of her mourning apparel was felt to be commensurate with the sublime status of her mourning self in the pantheon of Irish nationalism.

National mourning had long been a speciality with Maud Gonne. On 11 October, 1891, she put on mourning for Charles Stewart Parnell, whom she never seems to have met, and travelled on the boat that brought him back from Holyhead to Ireland. Yeats recalled meeting that boat on that "stormy October morning": "I had gone to Kingston [Kingstown] Pier to meet the Mail Boat that arrived about 6 am. I was expecting a friend, but met what I thought much less of at the time, the body of Parnell". The friend was of course Maud Gonne. Eleven years later, she was mourning for the Pope and against the King-Emperor, simultaneously.

In 1916, Maud was Cathleen ni Houlihan again, in real life or life in death, mourning not only John MacBride but also all who had died for Ireland in every generation. And she was also, as in 1902, calling for further blood-sacrifice.

It was above all Yeats's play that made possible this extraordinary comeback. *Cathleen ni Houlihan* was now central to the nationalist folk-memory, image by image and line by line, and it was never more alive than in 1916. Because it was so vividly and hauntingly alive, Maud Gonne's performance in it was that which was remembered about her, long after that performance, when other episodes of her chequered career had been forgotten. But it wasn't only the memory of that performance. Maud's own theatrical instinct was keen. She saw her opening, and when she made her entrance, she was dressed to perfection for her role in the 1916 real-life revival of *Cathleen ni Houlihan*. (A revival of the play had actually been scheduled for Easter Week 1916 but had to be cancelled because of the Rising.)

Yeats certainly had Maud's theatrical-political resurrection somewhat in mind, as well as her husband's death, when he wrote the famous lines in Easter, 1916:

All, all are changed, changed utterly
A terrible beauty is born.

Let us now step back ten years, to 1906; Maud Gonne as we have seen was then in the deepest trouble both with Catholics (as Catholics) and with nationalists (as nationalists). As her behaviour pattern had been designed to alienate the whole Protestant and unionist community, she had now become a pariah-figure for the whole of Irish society for the time being. And Yeats, with his eyes open, chose to share her isolation and unpopularity. Generously and courageously, he defended Maud Gonne – who had been hissed at Yeats's side in the Abbey Theatre – and defended her in the bitter controversy. In other circumstances, this expression of personal feeling, towards the woman he was known to have loved, might have been forgiven him. But not in the context of the quarrel between Maud Gonne and Major John MacBride. To take Maud Gonne's part in that quarrel was to lend yourself to the

British-abetted conspiracy to smear the greatest living nationalist hero. Yeats had had the militant Catholic-nationalists against him, since the beginning of the century. Over the Gonne-MacBride controversy he had all shades of nationalist and Catholic opinion against him.

THE PLAYBOY OF THE WESTERN WORLD

In these unpropitious circumstances, it was an act of high courage for Yeats to stage John Millington Synge's *The Playboy of the Western World* in the Abbey Theatre, where it opened in January 1907. The *Playboy* gave Yeats's Catholic-nationalist enemies their opportunity. For the first time a play in Yeats's theatre could be credibly attacked on both Catholic and nationalist grounds. The great emotional meeting-ground of the two is over chastity. If you are felt to impugn the chastity of Irish Catholic womanhood, you are besmirching the Catholic religion and the Irish nation, simultaneously. At that point the two jaws of the great Catholic-nationalist pincers close on the hapless calumniator.

As we have seen *The Leader* had tried this ploy out over *Diarmuid and Grainne* five years before. The picture of Grainne was held to be an insult to Irish womanhood. That attack had fizzled. That play is set in pre-Christian Ireland, and Grainne is therefore not a Catholic so the pincers didn't work. *The Playboy* is set in modern Ireland, in what is obviously a Catholic community. So if any of the women can be seen as deviating from the highest standards of sexual morality – including rigid decorum of speech – then that will be an insult to Irish Catholic womanhood, and an occasion for the pincers.

When the first riot broke out in the theatre, Yeats was in Aberdeen, where Lady Gregory telegraphed him: "Audience broke up in disorder at the word 'shift'" ("Shift", a female undergarment "aka chemise". Female undergarments were at this time felt to be unmentionable by a decent woman, in the presence of men.)

I doubt whether theatre riots are ever spontaneous and I

feel sure this one was not. I believe the organisers had chosen their ground carefully after seeing the play at its first night (which passed off without incident). The word "shift" was carefully chosen as the trigger for the riot, thus making it appear that the modesty of the Irish Catholic audience had been outraged (on this particular night . . .) by this gross insult to Irish Catholic womanhood and to the Irish nation.

The Leader's editorial comment on the affair (in its issue of 2 February, 1907) was surprisingly circumspect, which tends to confirm my opinion that DP Moran had had a hand in the planning of the riot. "Mr Synge", said the editorial, "has apparently outraged Irish piety and the authorities of the theatre are, we think unwise in fighting the cause of what they call 'freedom of judgement' with such a weapon as *The Playboy of the Western World.*"

The Leader's reviewer of the play, in the same issue, put the boot in:

"The unmistakable, vigorous and spontaneous outburst of disapproval which practically put an end to the last act of Mr Synge's gruesome farce at the Abbey Theatre last Saturday can only be regretted on the grounds that it was so long delayed . . . Attacks on filial affection, the sacredness of life and the modesty of women . . . an undercurrent of animalism and irreligion." *The Leader* warned that if there were any more of this, "criticism must eventually take the form of cabbage". At a later performance when there had been calls – or as *The Leader* claimed, a call – of "Kill the author," other newspapers protested against such incitement to murder. *The Leader* editorially deplored the fuss about what it called "that bantering and, under all the circumstances, we should say, rather witty remark" (16 February, 1907).

Yeats returned from Aberdeen to Dublin on receiving Lady Gregory's telegram. When new riots broke out he called in the police, who arrested some of the rioters. To call in the police to suppress a nationalist riot destroyed whatever remained of Yeats's nationalist credentials. It was useless for him to remind people of those credentials by saying, as he did: "The author of *Cathleen ni Houlihan* addresses you". This only reminded the audience of Maud Gonne, and made things worse.

What made the matter still worse, and more confusing, was that Maud Gonne, now herself a pariah to nationalists and defended only by Yeats, now reproved him, on nationalist grounds for being unkind to the rioters. On 7 May, 1906, three months after the riots, Maud Gonne wrote to Yeats, from Aix les Bains:

"And as to you Willie, we are such friends you will not misunderstand me when I say you have done such things as calling in the police & witnessing for the Crown that have given them [nationalists] cause to hate you & it is a healthy sign that they do . . . A few years ago you openly *approved* and I *organized* the rendering impossible of English plays that we objected to on National grounds, in the theatres and music halls in Dublin. You start a theatre you call a *National* Theatre, in the beginning at all events it was to be a theatre for the people – you put on a play they consider wrong. Naturally they look on it as their duty to stop that play & the men who were fined, many of them I know to be very good and earnest young fellows, feel proud that they have suffered for the national cause."[41]

After January, 1907, Yeats's career ceases to be instructive in relation to the interaction of Catholicism and nationalism since, from the moment of these arrests, Yeats was no longer felt by Irish nationalists to be any sort of nationalist ("give them cause to hate you"). But this last phase of Yeats's involvement in populist nationalism, with the Gonne-MacBride controversy, has been probably the most illuminating of all, with regard to the working of that interaction.

From *The Leader*'s point of view, the *Playboy* affair was a victory. DP Moran's aim, in a campaign which lasted over seven years, had been to destroy Yeats's influence on Nationalist Ireland. Moran could certainly feel he had accomplished

---

41. *Gonne-MacBride Letters*, pp. 239-241. Most of these good and earnest young men at this time were heartily cursing Maud Gonne for smearing the national hero, Major John MacBride.

that, after Yeats had called in the police to suppress a nationalist riot. Nationalists had now seen the feet of clay of the man whom Catholics had always suspected. This was a closing of Catholic and nationalist ranks: very satisfactory to Moran and *The Leader*.

IRISH IRELAND AS WEST BRITAIN

Yet in other ways the movement that *The Leader* represented – Irish Ireland – was in deep trouble, by the middle of the first decade of the twentieth century. The trouble was ideological, intellectual and moral, and involved significant psychological disturbance, as we shall see. And it was a trouble that was to continue to affect Irish nationalism long after *The Leader* had ceased to be a significant factor on the national scene. Where *The Leader* is useful to us today, in this matter as in others, is that it shows what is going on in the national psyche in a clearer light than other sources do.

The trouble had to do with the question of the revival of Gaelic – "the Irish language" as Irish Irelanders, and nationalists in general, invariably referred to it. For Irish Irelanders, the revival of the Irish language was a paramount necessity, at the very centre of their movement; in theory. In this regard there was seminal significance, for Irish Irelanders, in a paper by Douglas Hyde: "The necessity of de-Anglicising Ireland". All Irish Irelanders agreed on the necessity for this. In particular, de-Anglicising Ireland was what *The Leader* saw as its mission.

But – and it was a very big "but" indeed – the project that Hyde had identified as central to de-Anglicising Ireland – the revival of the Irish language – was not happening. That it was not happening on a national scale was not surprising. The metamorphosis of Ireland from an almost-entirely-English-speaking country (by the end of the nineteenth century) to an Irish-speaking one would clearly take time: if it happened at all, which it didn't. More disturbing, in relation to the character of Irish Ireland, was a specific facet of the non-revival: *even among most Irish Irelanders, Irish was not being revived.* This fact is manifest from the files of *The Leader* itself. *The Leader* starts out as an almost-entirely English-language weekly, with one article in Gaelic. This would be reasonable for starters, but if *The Leader* and its contributors and readers were serious about reviving what they called the Irish language, we would have expected the proportion of the use of Irish to expand over time. It didn't. *The Leader* remained throughout its existence a weekly periodical almost entirely in the English language, making only token use of Irish.

There were Irish Irelanders, like my mother, who showed their seriousness about what they regarded as the Irish language, by taking the trouble to learn that language properly: speaking, reading and writing it with ease. But these were few in number and always remained so. Most Irish Irelanders were content to express their detestation of everything English in the only language which they actually knew, which was English. And this was not peculiar to the particular period we are now looking at, or to the narrow circle associated with a particular periodical. This was to be a standing feature of Irish nationalism throughout the twentieth century.

All the political parties in the Republic of Ireland are devoted to the revival of the Irish language, in theory. The largest party, Fianna Fáil, is committed to two "national aims": the revival of Irish, and the unification of Ireland. (I shall be discussing unification later). Irish is defined as "the first official language" in the Irish Constitution (1937) the work of the founder of Fianna Fáil, Eamon de Valera. English is the second official language. The Constitution was actually written in English and translated into Irish. Yet where there appears to be a contradiction between the two versions, the translation is to prevail over the original. Yet the second official language is the one the actual Irish people use in every transaction of their daily lives. Even in the Dáil itself, and even among Fianna Fáil deputies, the second official language is the one that is actually used.

To have high esteem for a language you don't actually use,

while holding the one you actually do use in low esteem, is to be in a parlous mental and moral condition and that indeed has been the condition of Irish nationalism for most of the twentieth century.

For an illustration of how parlous, and even pathological, the condition can get, we can look again to the files of *The Leader*, that window of unique explicitness into the nationalist mind. From 31 October, 1908 to 23 January, 1909, *The Leader* ran a series of articles devoted to the topic: "Is the English language poisonous?" "Poisonous" was defined as poisonous to Faith and Patriotism. (If it was poisonous to Faith, the bishops and priests of Ireland must have been poisoning the faithful, for the language of the Catholic Church in Ireland was then English, as it remains today). One contributor confesses to doubt about the answer to that question. The others had no doubt: English *was* poisonous. All those who were of that opinion expressed themselves in English, and only in English. None felt it necessary to explain why they themselves were using this putatively toxic medium of communication. Nor did *The Leader* itself admit any concern about its own responsibility in distributing poisonous material, week after week, to all its readers.

Irish cultural nationalism is a rum business: probably the rummest form of cultural nationalism that has ever existed anywhere.

Irish Irelanders consistently denounced other Irish people for being Anglicised: West British. Yet they themselves (in great majority) remained Anglicised in the most basic particular: that of tongue. That is to say, by their own criteria, taken seriously, they were themselves West British: "Far West British", perhaps.

CULTURAL AND TERRITORIAL NATIONALISM

The "revival of Irish" project was one that had a tendency to divide Irish Catholicism from Irish nationalism, not to unite them. Irish Irelanders sometimes tried, however, to associate the two, in relation to Irish. One way of doing this was by attributing the decline of the Irish language to "souperism": "the Souper movement in the past did much to kill Irish". (*The Leader*, 19 April, 1902). Another way was to suggest that an Ireland which was totally Irish-speaking would be immune to the immoral and irreligious influences carried in to Ireland by the English language. A pamphlet said to be written by "A Priest", carried the self-explanatory title: *Irish or Infidelity – Which?* (advertised in *The Leader* 28 August, 1909). The Catholic Church was not however, buying this stuff. The Church had made its peace – since 1886 – with constitutional political nationalism. But it could *not* (as a body) accept a cultural nationalism which aimed to replace the English language by Irish. The influence of the Irish Catholic Church on world Catholicism – which was a major influence – was exerted exclusively through English. The influence of Irish priests and religious on Catholicism in the United States and Canada, and in Australia and New Zealand, and even in India and Africa, was very great, and dependent entirely on the use of English. And the influence of the Irish Catholic Church in Rome, which was significant, was based on Irish influence in the English-speaking world. "Ireland's Spiritual Empire" is a grandiose phrase, but it does stand for a reality, which is more than can be said for Irish cultural nationalism.

Over the language revival project, Catholicism and nationalism were in divergence, but it wasn't a serious divergence, because most nationalists were not serious about the revival project, as the results showed. Nationalists had settled for the *cúpla focal* and the *cúpla focal* did not endanger Ireland's Spiritual Empire.[42]

But the conditions arising from the failure of the revival project – a failure which, of course, has never been officially acknowledged – were propitious to a new convergence between Catholicism and nationalism.

---

42. *Cúpla focal*: A couple of words, in Gaelic. The *cúpla focal* are thrown in from time to time, in order to sanitise the speaker's habitual use of the language which he is supposed to be determined to replace. The *cúpla focal* are the core of Fianna Fáil culture.

The reason for the new convergence was not just the silent removal of what had been a bone of contention (and would have been a major bone of contention if the revival project had developed successfully). There was more to the new convergence than that. It was, and is, a convergence of *aims*. The unacknowledged failure of cultural nationalism left the field to political nationalism. The objective of Irish political nationalism during most of the twentieth century – since 1922 – has been what is called "the reunification of the national territory" by which is meant the extinction of Northern Ireland as a distinct political entity, and the incorporation of its territory into a united Ireland.

Now, in proportion to the failure of cultural nationalism, territorial nationalism rose in importance. You will recall that the two "national aims" of Fianna Fáil are the restoration of the Irish language as the language spoken by the Irish people, and the reunification of Ireland. Most people know and have known for a long time – that the first aim, restoration of the Irish language – is unfulfillable. This makes efforts to achieve the second aim – reunification – all the dearer to the hearts of Fianna Fáil people. No one – not even a Fianna Fáil TD – likes having to admit to himself (even if only to himself) that he is a *total* fraud; as would be the case if *both* national aims were (even privately) acknowledged to be fraudulent. So, "ending partition" became the core-value of Fianna Fáil. And Fianna Fáil is itself the core of modern Irish nationalism.

Now, the majority of the population of Northern Ireland are Protestants, and the reason for their refusal to be incorporated in a united Ireland is that they would become a minority among (or, as they think, *under*) the Catholic majority in the island of Ireland. The dispute over Northern Ireland is therefore a dispute over territory between Catholics and Protestants. This is where the convergence comes in. Irish Catholic nationalists relate to the dispute in both their capacities. As nationalists, they resent Northern Ireland as an alien intrusion. As Catholics, they resent Protestant power in what was once Catholic territory. As Catholic nationalists, they resent both. I shall come back to this.

The Catholic Church, discreetly but sedulously, supports the campaign for reunification, and quietly exerts its influence against the amendment of Articles 2 and 3. I saw an example of this in action in the late 1960's when I was a member of a Dáil committee on the possible amendment of Articles 2 and 3. All the Protestant Churches had made submissions in favour of the removal of the territorial claim. Then Cardinal Conway, Archbishop of Armagh and Primate of All Ireland, appeared before us. The Protestant claims were unfounded he said, since the Articles in question merely express an aspiration, not a territorial claim. I was sitting beside the Cardinal, and I had with me a copy of the Constitution, open at Articles 2 and 3. I laid the document before him drawing his attention to the definition of "the national territory" (in Article 2) as consisting of "the whole island of Ireland, its islands and the territorial seas". The Cardinal neither replied nor looked at the text. He just took the copy of the Constitution between finger and thumb and tossed it, in a graceful arc, to a distant corner of the Committee room. This was not an angry gesture; the Cardinal was quite calm. This was just his way of signalling that the argument was over, and that he had won. The Committee took the hint and did not recommend any change in the Articles.

This convergence of Catholicism and nationalism, over territory, did not begin to operate fully until Northern Ireland had come into existence. But the ground for that convergence was being prepared, in the first decade-and-a-half of the century, with the failure of cultural nationalism, and the growing power of political nationalism. We shall have to deal, in the next section, with the more virulent strain of political nationalism which from 1913 on – and especially after 1916 – superseded both the mainstream constitutional nationalism and the more aggressive cultural-political and sectarian nationalism of Irish Ireland, expressed in *The Leader*. The nationalism that became dominant after 1916 was officially non-sectarian and anti-sectarian. The official rhetoric of nationalism after 1916 was altogether free from sectarianism. Indeed the official rhetoric of mainstream Irish nationalism has *always* been free from sectarianism. The great value of DP Moran's *The Leader* is that it allows us to watch, from 1900 to 1914, some of the forces at work *beneath* the official rhetoric. It would be a mistake to assume that these forces disappeared from the culture (after 1916), when all we know is that their public expression came to be discountenanced by the leadership of the newly-dominant school of nationalism. And as we shall see, the professions of non-sectarianism are belied by the actual pattern of modern nationalist activity in relation to Northern Ireland.

The present generation of nationalist leaders are far too politically correct to use the crudely sectarian terminology in which DP Moran revelled. What they are trying to do is to twist the Sourfaces out of control over Northern Ireland. Only they don't put it that way. They say they are "working for an agreed Ireland", and look and sound as if butter wouldn't melt in their mouths. It is possible in the late twentieth century to feel, in a way, a certain nostalgia for the world of DP Moran. At least the old brute usually said what he meant, and said it right out. No modern Irish nationalist leader even finds it possible to conceive of associating intention with utterance in this way. Their vocal chords, which are extremely active, are permanently disconnected from their thinking process. I shall be offering some examples of this phenomenon, later in this study.

THE BEGINNING OF PARTITION

When the Home Rule crisis opened, in the second decade of the twentieth century, the Ulster Protestants mobilised against the Third Home Rule Bill, first politically, then militarily. Irish nationalists at first refused to take this seriously. The Protestants were bluffing. They were not any kind of autonomous force at all. They were wholly dependent on England, and would have to do whatever England told them to do. That was in their monetary interest, and they had no loyalty higher than that. As Tim Healy had wittily put it, they were loyal not to the Crown, but the half-crown.

Irish nationalists were betrayed by their own contemptuous image of their opponent. This often happens with nationalists – compare Arab contempt, in the run-up to 1948, for the capacity of Israel to resist; or German contempt for American military capability in two world wars. In all three cases, there was a religious-racist component in the fatal underestimation of the opponent. (Religious and racial hostility are not totally discrete phenomena as some seem to assume: consider the Spanish Inquisition's concept of purity of blood, *limpieza de sangre*, as a religious requirement. The contagion of heresy was genetically transmitted and had to be eliminated by fire. Consider also DP Moran's racist portrait of the Sourfaces).

Ulster Protestants became notorious for blatant sectarianism, and some of them have richly earned that reputation. But it is the blatancy that is unique about them in Ireland, not the sectarianism. Not all Irish Catholics are sectarian, just as not all Ulster Protestants are. But a good many, in both communities, are sectarian and the sectarian bitterness is evenly distributed, contrary to appearances.

The difference is that the Catholics, having been historically the underdogs, are much better at dissimulating their sectarianism. A few have become virtuosos in this type of dissimulation. I can think of one leading Catholic – John Hume – whose actual attitude to Ulster Protestants is the implacable and relentless hostility of the seventeenth century, yet who has come to be regarded by innocent English and Americans as a paragon of oecumenical enlightenment, forever in quest of peace with his Protestant neighbours, and forever being rebuffed by their archaic and incomprehensible intransigence and bigotry.

After that necessary digression, let us now return, briefly, to the Home Rule crisis of 1911 to 1914. When it became apparent that Ulster Protestants would not willingly enter a Home Rule Ireland, Irish nationalists insisted that it was the constitutional duty of the British Government to oblige the Protestants to accept Home Rule. The word "coerce" was not used (see above, "dissimulation") but that was most certainly the idea ("persuade" is the euphemism in use in 1994). The British declined, for adequate reasons: British public opinion would never have approved the use of force to induce people who wanted to remain in the United Kingdom, to leave its jurisdiction.

Once the British rejected the use of force, partition was inevitable. Irish nationalists, of all descriptions, saw this as a British cave-in before naked force. There were marked gradations of feeling about this, among nationalists of different shades, but the general idea was common to all. No nationalist, at that time, saw the unionist claim to local self-determination as representing any kind of moral force. Any Protestant claim to morality was suspect in Catholic eyes (and of course *vice versa*).

In response to the political victory of the Ulster Volunteers, Irish nationalists set up their own, overwhelmingly Catholic, militia: the Irish Volunteers. The materials for a political-sectarian civil war, in the entire island, were now in place. That is what would have happened then, if the British had disengaged, and if the British were to disengage now (in 1994), that is also what would happen.

Instead, what happened in August 1914, was the outbreak of the First World War, or more precisely the entry into that War of the whole United Kingdom, including all Ireland. Both constitutional nationalists and unionists, who a month earlier had appeared to be on the verge of being at one another's throats were now, if not united, at least arrayed on the same side. That Irish unionists would rally to the side of the United Kingdom, when threatened by a foreign enemy, was entirely in accordance with their whole tradition. But that Irish nationalists should support the British war-effort in 1914 has to seem extraordinary, in the retrospect of modern Irish nationalism, powerfully conditioned as that retrospect is, both by the events of 1916, and the subsequent cult of

Pearsean nationalism. But the political nationalism of most Irish people, in 1914, was not remotely Pearsean. In retrospect, the decision to support the war-effort has been vaguely personalised as "Redmond's tragic mistake." But there was nothing personal about it. The whole Irish Parliamentary Party supported the war-effort and there seems to have been no division on the subject, in 1914-15, among the Party's grassroots membership. The Catholic Church, as a whole, supported the war.[43] Nationalist Irishmen enlisted in the war-effort in approximately the same proportions as unionists did. This phenomenon cannot be accounted for just by John Redmond's charisma, which was not in fact particularly noticeable.

Another explanation, which was pushed at the end of the war by Sinn Féin, was that the Irish people were duped by the promise of Home Rule for after the war, not realising that this would be Home Rule *with partition*. In reality, the fact that Home Rule Ireland would be less than thirty-two counties was already well known in 1914. Some nationalists were furious about this; all were disappointed. It is clear that only a minority, at this point, resented it sufficiently to refuse to support the war effort. It would, after all, be Home Rule for where the great majority of them lived.

No personal or trivialising hypothesis will serve to explain a mass-phenomenon of the magnitude, and apparently paradoxical character, of Irish Catholic and nationalist support for the British war effort in 1914. There is only one hypothesis that can account for the phenomenon, and this is that most Irish Catholics and nationalists at this time were more pro-British, than they were anti-British. And this in turn can be largely accounted for by changes in religious and national alignments, over the previous generation.

For a significant minority of Irishmen, important for the future, the Manichean picture offered by the Christian

---

43. See David W Miller, "The Roman Catholic Church in Ireland, 1898 to 1918;" in Alan O'Day [ed] *Reactions to Irish Nationalism, 1865-1914* (Dublin, 1987); p.197

Brothers, and some others (with the encouragement of the same Bishops who supported the war), of wicked Protestant England oppressing virtuous Catholic Ireland, had an enduring appeal. But for most Irish Catholics, at the beginning of the second decade of our century, it clearly didn't fit the modern realities they knew. William Ewart Gladstone who had disestablished the [Anglican] Church of Ireland, and gone on to offer two Home Rule Bills, had been more popular in Catholic Ireland (and therefore more *un*popular in Protestant Ireland) than any Irish politician of the nineteenth century, with the exceptions of O'Connell and (up to 1891) Parnell. By 1914 the British Liberals and the Irish nationalists had been allies for more than a generation, since 1886. The Liberal alliance had brought benefits to Ireland, both when the Liberals were in office and when they were not. The Tory policy of "killing Home Rule by kindness" had changed the face of rural Ireland, in the first decade of the new century, mainly by great measures of land purchase, enabling the tenants to buy out the landlords.

All in all, most Irish nationalists in 1914 must have been reasonably satisfied with Home-Rule-with-partition-and-within-the-Empire, or they would not have reacted as they did to the British declaration of war against Imperial Germany. The fact that the occasion of the war was German aggression against a small Catholic nation – Belgium – helped the emotional climate, but it could not have been decisive had not the mood of nationalist Ireland, at that time, been favourable, on the whole, to Britain. Yet even in the minds of those moderate nationalists, in 1914, there must have been an atavistic undercurrent, that could not be *all that* favourable to Britain. Inside any given Irish nationalist, in the moment of according support to the British war effort, or enlisting in the British Army, there must have been, as it were, a little Christian Brother, screaming to be let out. Two years later, he did get out, and he is still at large.

MYSTICAL NATIONALISM: PATRICK PEARSE

At a time when the elected representatives of the Irish people were declaring their support for the British war-effort, a very small select non-elected group, the Irish Republican Brotherhood (aka, "Fenians"), was deciding that, at some time during this war, a blow must be struck against Britain. The timing of the rebellion was left to be decided later. In the meantime, an agitation was to be launched both against the war-effort, and against those who were deemed to have betrayed the Irish nationalist cause, by supporting the war-effort. The pivotal figure in that agitation, and also the man who was eventually to determine the timing of the 1916 Rising, was one of the most extraordinary and charismatic personalities of the twentieth century: Patrick Pearse.

It was in the period between the Home Rule crises of 1913 and Easter 1916 that the fusion of Catholicism and Irish nationalism attained its maximum intensity in the psyche of Patrick Pearse, the most notable product of the Irish Christian Brothers. Pearse's father was English (a convert to Catholicism), his mother an Irish Catholic[43(a)]. A Freudian might discern an oedipal motivation. Less conjecturally, to be the son of an Englishman and to be exposed to the concentrated Anglophobia of Christian Brothers' history lessons (and more diffuse Anglophobia in other subjects) must have been a traumatic experience. Barry Coldrey records an episode which may have been decisive in the formation of Pearse's nationalism. It is, at any rate clear, from the nature of the episode itself, that the atmosphere of Pearse's home had not (during his boyhood) been that of Irish Ireland. The episode consisted of a disconcerting encounter between the boy Pearse and one of his teachers, Brother Canice Craven. Coldrey describes Craven as "a much more advanced and outspoken nationalist than most contemporary Christian Brothers". This makes him a blazing nationalist indeed. In the

---

43a. For details of James Pearse's politics, see Ruth Dudley Edwards, *Patrick Pearse: the Triumph of Failure* (London, 1977), chapter 1

year of Pearse's death, Craven was to become editor of the ultra-nationalist ultra-Catholic and Anglophobic *Our Boys*, and remained editor until 1929. What may have been the crucial encounter between Pearse and Craven is told by Coldrey as follows:

"One revealing incident involving both Craven and Pearse occurred on an occasion when Craven set his class an essay on 'The Importance of Sea Power'. Pearse could write a good essay, and he was asked to read his composition to the class. When he came to the sentence 'Our navy today sails the seven seas, supreme and unchallenged', Craven glanced at the writer and informed the class that England used its naval power to plunder the rest of the world and Ireland as well. Pearse never forgot this lesson and referred to it in later conversation with other Brothers."[44]

It must have been a searing experience for the young Pearse to be thus rebuked, in the presence of the class, for words he must have heard from his father's lips.

Owen Dudley Edwards, who gave me invaluable help with this text, demurred at the above, which as originally drafted referred to "a sentence" Pearse must have heard etc. He wrote; "No, no. There's no 'he must' about it. 'He must' only because you want him to. The Pearses subscribed to Victorian magazines, notably the enjoyable and violently imperialist *Little Folks* . . . Since we know he read those bound volumes and we know they contained this guff about our navy, and we know sweet Fanny Adams about what his daddy told him, *Little Folks* is a much better source than Dad for the navy".

Normally, I gratefully, and usually silently, go along with Owen's proposed emendations, from which I have learned and profited a great deal. But I can only go a small part of the way with this one. Having reflected on the objection I changed "a sentence" to "words". It seems to me virtually certain that Pearse would have heard the words "our navy" from his father. Pearse's father was English. If his conversion to Catholicism implied any kind of conversion to Irish nationalism, it would have been to Home Rule, under which

---

44. Barry Coldrey, *Faith and Fatherland*, p. 254

defence would have been reserved to the Imperial Parliament and a good Home Ruler could still refer to "our Navy". The fact adduced by Owen himself – the family subscription to *Little Folk* – shows that Pearse's father considered a "violently imperalist" magazine suitable reading for his young son. The British Navy was a main topic of discussion in the English-speaking world on the eve of the First World War. I believe that the young Pearse not merely heard the phrase "our navy" on his father's lips – how else could an average Englishman refer to the force in question? – but that he must have heard it with very much the same emotional connotations as attached to it in *Little Folks*, and in Patrick Pearse's own essay.

The point in dispute is far more than a trivial or pedantic one. If I am right – and readers will make up their own minds on that – this incident in Brother Craven's classroom was a turning point in the life of Patrick Pearse, and therefore in the history of the Irish people. Brother Craven was telling the boy, by implication, that he must repudiate, not merely the world of *Little Folks* but *his own father* who inhabited that world and subscribed to it. Personally, I cannot imagine a more traumatic moment in the education of a boy. Pearse forsook his father's world for Brother Craven's at the Brother's bidding. The subsequent fervour of Pearse's commitment to Brother Craven's world was proportionate, I believe, to the pain of that conversion.[45]

Up to the Home Rule crisis of 1913, Pearse's nationalism though "advanced" did not appear as exceptional. He identified with the Irish Ireland movement (discussed above) and when he founded his school, St. Enda's, in 1908, he ran a series of advertisements in the August and September issues of *The Leader*, describing St. Enda's as:

"An Irish-Ireland School for Catholic Boys
Sgoil Ghaedhealach le h-aghaigh Gaedheal Óg"

---

45. *Faith and Fatherland*, p. 255. Another Brother believed that Pearse in "afterlife was influenced by what he had been listening to in that old schoolroom". For an account of specifically Irish rural and folk influences present in Pearse's childhood home see Edwards, *Pearse*, p. 8

(The description in Gaelic means simply "Gaelic School for young Gaels". The word Catholic does not appear. But a Gaelic identity of Catholicity and Gaelicism is assumed. The normal Gaelic term for the local Protestant Church is an *teampall gallda*: the foreign church).

"Irish Ireland" meant constitutional nationalist, with an emphasis on the Irish language, and this was clearly Pearse's position up to 1913. But in that year, it began to appear that the constitutional nationalist project might be blocked "by force" and nationalists began to consider, and be excited about, some kind of counter-force. In January, 1913, the Ulster Unionist Council decided to set up the Ulster Volunteer Force. Faced with this threat, the mood of Irish nationalism attained a new intensity among some young Irish Irelanders: a mood not shared by most Irish nationalists in this period, as support for the war showed. In Pearse, rising nationalism took a mystical form, fusing nationalism and Catholicism.

SACRALISED WOLFE TONE

Pearse delivered an address at the grave of Wolfe Tone, in Bodenstown Churchyard, Co. Kildare on 22 June, 1913. The address opens with the words:

"We have come to the holiest place in Ireland; holier even than the place where Patrick sleeps in Down. Patrick brought us life, but this man died for us. He was the greatest of Irish Nationalists . . . We have come to renew our adhesion to the faith of Tone: to express once more our full acceptance of the gospel of Irish Nationalism which he was the first to formulate in worldly terms. This man's soul was a burning flame, so ardent so generous so pure, that to come into communion with it is to come unto a new baptism, into a new regeneration and cleansing."[46]

"Gospel of Irish nationalism . . . communion . . . baptism . . . regeneration."

---

46. *Collected Works of Padraic H. Pearse: Political Writings and Speeches*. Phoenix Co. Ltd. Dublin, Cork, Belfast (no date) pp. 58-62

Pearse is now fully launched on his project of raising nationalism, in himself and in others, to a far higher emotional pitch by sacralising it, and fusing it with the religious faith of the people. There is a tragic irony in the sacralisation of Wolfe Tone, in particular. Wolfe Tone – as Pearse well knew, but chose to ignore – was a child of the eighteenth-century Enlightenment. His hope for Ireland was that Enlightenment values would come to supplant what he regarded as superstitious beliefs – of Catholics, Protestants and Dissenters – and the animosities begotten by these. Tone greatly overestimated the extent to which Enlightenment values had come to prevail in the Ireland of his time. But he may have been right in thinking that the weakening of the religious creeds, through Enlightenment, had the potential of weakening also the religious animosities which attached to the creeds. One should not make too much of that; there were plenty of other sources of animosity. But the religious sources of such feelings are among the most powerful and easily identifiable. At least Tone's project was intended to lead the Irish away from the civil war continually counselled by those ancestral voices. By a horrible irony, the United Irish Movement actually *precipitated* a civil war in 1798. That was a result, in part at least, of hubris: a gross overestimation of the extent to which United Irish ideas – as understood by Tone and his middle-class friends – had spread among the population at large. That and an underestimation of the power of those ancestral voices. But in the longer term, the ideas of Tone – the eighteenth-century Tone, not Pearse's creation – had a tendency to put a brake on sectarianism.

Sacralised Wolfe Tone – Wolfe Tone presiding over a Catholic nationalist pantheon as conceived by a Catholic mystic – has a quite different meaning. Tone is turned into a Catholic tribal icon to be carried into the coming battle with the Ulster Protestants. That is not how Pearse sees it, of course. He sees it as his mission to complete the work of Tone. But note how he formulates "the work of Tone" (in the same Bodenstown address): "Protestant and Dissenter must be brought into amity with Catholics". No suggestion of the other way round. The Catholic position is thought of as fixed, and it is the Protestants who *must* move in the direction the Catholics want. Pearse's Tone is thought of as a kind of convert to basic Irish Catholicism: Pearse, in this same address, tells of " . . . how this heretic toiled to make free men of Catholic helots, how as he worked among them, he grew to know and to love the real, the historic Irish people." So it is the Catholics who are real and historical, and the Protestants who are unreal and unhistorical . . . This is Pearse, not Tone.

Having sacralised Wolfe Tone, Pearse goes on to give Robert Emmet the same treatment. In an address delivered at the Emmet Commemoration in the Academy of Music, Brooklyn, New York, on 26 March, 1914[47] Pearse refers to patriotism as "a faith which is of the same nature as religious faith". He describes Emmet's death as "a sacrifice Christ-like in its perfection . . . such a death always means a redemption". John Mitchel joins Wolfe Tone and Emmet in the Pearsean pantheon. Mitchel's *Jail Journal* is "the last Gospel of the New Testament of Irish nationalism as Wolfe Tone's *Autobiography* is the first".[48]

All three of the sacralised nationalists belong to Protestant families. Sacralisation takes them out of their Protestant (or post-Protestant or Enlightenment) context. But it is not exactly a question of Catholicising them. Pearse's fusion of Catholicism and nationalism is not (by 1913) the Catholic nationalism that was general in the Irish Ireland of 1900 to 1912 and preached in *The Leader. That* Catholic nationalism was religiously orthodox, and so put Catholicism first. Pearse's mystical nationalism puts nationalism first. This is implicit in placing Wolfe Tone above St Patrick. It also appears in that Bodenstown address where Pearse said: "When men come to a graveyard they pray: and each of us prays in our heart. But we do not pray for Tone – men who died that their people

---

47. *Collected Works* etc. pp. 64 – 75
48. "From a Hermitage"; (Reissued 1915) *Collected Works* pp. 139-212

may be free 'have no need for prayer'."

The last five words are of course a quotation from Yeats's *Cathleen ni Houlihan*.[49] We may be sure that his audience recognised the quotation. This doctrine of nationalist salvation has peculiar point and poignancy in relation to Tone. For orthodox Catholics, at this time, there was no *point* in praying for Tone, since Tone committed suicide, and suicide was then held to incur automatic damnation. But Pearse, in the name of a nationalist counter-orthodoxy, lays down, with equal dogmatic certitude, that Tone is automatically saved, because he died for Ireland.

Pearse is not – by 1913 – a Catholic nationalist of any ordinary type. He is a nationalist first; where Catholic doctrine conflicts with nationalism, nationalism must prevail. But Pearse's nationalism, however refractory to Catholic orthodoxy in one particular area, is thoroughly permeated by Catholic devotional feeling.

The statements of Pearse we have been considering were all made before the outbreak of the First World War. This was a period of growing nationalist excitement throughout Europe (especially in the Balkans) and exalted nationalism was finding expression in many countries. Pearse was not unique in this. Even his fusion of nationalism and Catholicism was not quite unique. In France, Charles Péguy (1873-1914) was an ardent nationalist and Catholic, whose nationalism was not amenable to orthodox censure or control, as we have seen.

Pearse's fusion of nationalism and Catholicism was not unique in itself, but I know of no other case where such a fusion declared itself in so intense a form, and in such a sustained manner, as it did in the case of Pearse from 1913 to Pearse's intentional death in 1916, entirely motivated by the fusion in question.

---

49. The Old Woman said "have no need of prayers". Pearse is quoting from memory.

PEARSE PREPARES FOR THE RISING

After the United Kingdom of Great Britain and Ireland (as it then was) went to war with the Central Powers, in August, 1914, Pearse's nationalist writings undergo a subtle change. They become more purposeful; they are part of a preparation. As we have seen, the Irish Republican Brotherhood, of which Pearse had now become a leading member, had determined on an insurrection at some time during the course of the war, in accordance with Wolfe Tone's principle, "England's difficulty is Ireland's opportunity". It was not until near the end of 1915 that the date of the Rising was set, for Easter, 1916. It was at this time that Pearse wrote the pamphlet *Ghosts*, the preface of which is quoted in the epigraph of this book: "There is only one way to appease a ghost, you must do the thing it asks you. The ghosts of a nation sometimes ask very big things; and they must be appeased at whatever the cost."[50] The conclusion of this pamphlet makes it clear that what the ghosts are asking for, and must have, is blood . . . "An aspiration of King David haunts my memory when I think on Ireland and her wrongs:

That thy foot may be dipped in the blood of thine enemies, and that the tongue of thy dogs may be red through the same."

(Pearse's italics). Pearse goes on: "Thus Tone, thus Davis, thus Lalor, thus Parnell. Methinks I have raised some ghosts that will take a little laying".[51]

The dating of the Preface to *Ghosts* is clearly not fortuitous, but felicitously timed, with the liturgical year in mind. The

---

50. *Ghosts* in *Collected Works* etc pp. 223-255
51. None of the Irish patriots whom Pearse cites actually spoke or wrote in this vein. But their ghosts do so speak, to Pearse, and through him.

next great feast in the Christian year will be Easter, 1916, the date already decided on as the time of the Irish Rising: the "very big thing" asked by the ghosts who "must be appeased".

Ghosts is the first of what turned out to be a series of four pamphlets. The other three are: *The Separatist Idea* (1 Feb. 1916); *The Spiritual Nation* (13 Feb. 1916) and *The Sovereign People* (31 March, 1916). The four form "a continuous argument" in Pearse's mind: a sort of spiritual-political testament. Much of the argument is devoted to a highly idiosyncratic interpretation of Irish history, and is not directly relevant to our subject-matter here. In most of this, his last body of writings, Pearse seems to be holding in check, to some extent, the expression of his personal mystical nationalism to which he had given such free vent in the year before the outbreak of war. Pearse was now part of a collective enterprise, and the nationalism of his colleagues had not been accustomed to mystical expression. But the last pamphlet of all, *The Sovereign People,* contains the last and most apocalyptic expression of Pearse's identification of the Irish [Catholic] nation with Jesus Christ:

"Let no man be mistaken as to who will be lord in Ireland when Ireland is free. The people will be lord and master. The people who wept in Gethsemane, who trod the sorrowful way, who died naked on a cross, who went down into hell, will rise again glorious and immortal, will sit on the right hand of God, who will come in the end to give judgement, a judge just and terrible".[52]

At first sight, the above passage seems crazy, and wildly remote from anything that happened in post-1916 (and post-1922) Ireland. But if we look at it in the context of Pearsean values, as expressed in the general body of his work, we can see that it makes sense, and may even be prophetically accurate, though the prophecy is esoteric and conveyed through mystical hyperbole, and has yet to be fully realised, if it ever is.

---

52. *Collected Works* p. 345

First of all, what is this "people" who "will be lord and master"? Not just any Tom Dick and Harry, certainly. Pearse was not a democrat, and had the utmost contempt for those who were chosen by democratic process to represent the Irish Catholic people in Pearse's lifetime (the Irish Parliamentary Party). Pearse's ideas of choice and representation are quite different from the prosaic democratic ones. For Pearse, "the people", in the ordinary sense, meaning the general mass of the population, does exist and has a limited sacral sense, in constituting a storehouse of suffering. And in the Pearsean system, they are to be represented. But they are not to choose their representatives; they are not fit to do that. This is an aristocratic system, featuring a service élite. Those who represent the people are summoned from above, by a personified Ireland (aka Cathleen ni Houlihan) to avenge the sufferings of the people and preferably to die in the attempt to avenge these sufferings. At the apex of the Pearsean system is the hero and martyr, Theobald Wolfe Tone.

"The voice of the people" has thus a quite different meaning for Pearse, to the meaning commonly attached to it. Pearse says of Tone (in the Bodenstown Address) that he "made articulate the dumb voices of the centuries". It is the voices made articulate by Tone, and made even more articulate by Pearse – transmitting the summons of Cathleen ni Houlihan – which determine not only who shall represent the people, but actually who shall *be* the people. (The people, in the sense of the populace at large, being inert.) It is a kind of representation by incarnation.

The people "who will be lord and master in Ireland when Ireland is free" will be those who have obeyed the summoning voices of certain privileged ghosts: 'ghosts of dead men that have bequeathed a trust to us living men . . . ghosts of a nation'. At the time when Pearse wrote *The Sovereign People* those ghosts had asked of Pearse and his comrades "Very big things": nothing less than armed insurrection, which would certainly be crushed by the overwhelming military power which it had to challenge. It is inconceivable that Pearse would have included as part of "the lord and master", in the new Ireland, any persons who had failed to obey the summons of the ghosts.

When Pearse writes of the passion and crucifixion of "the people" what he has to have in mind, in these the last days he knows he has to live, are the sufferings and death he knows to be in store for himself, and for an unknown number of his comrades, because they have chosen to suffer. What he had in mind by "the resurrection" was a new and purified Ireland, under the benign authority of those who had been cleansed and purified by participation in insurrection.

Pearse and his comrades did not, of course, intend that the Easter Rising by itself should be conclusive. It was to be sacrificial, and to stimulate further insurrections, until Ireland should be altogether free. The coming Ireland would be ruled by a kind of coalition, consisting of the survivors of the insurrections, together with the ghosts of those who died in them, and in earlier insurrections. Wolfe Tone would be there and Robert Emmet, John Mitchel and also Patrick Pearse, James Connolly and the other signatories of the Proclamation. If any survivors should falter, the ghosts would be there to address them and correct them.

The prophecy has not been fulfilled – since Ireland is not yet free, as Pearse and his comrades understood freedom – but neither has it been falsified. The Irish State which came into being in 1921 and which took the name of the Republic of Ireland is not the Republic proclaimed in 1916, but it is generally thought of by nationalists (first by Michael Collins, later by Eamon de Valera) as a stage towards the attainment of that Republic. And the actual (or interim) Republic was dominated, in terrestrial terms, by the survivors of the insurrections of 1916 and of 1919-22. And the ghosts of those who perished in those insurrections had a certain power over those survivors. Some of the survivors grew restive in relation to that power (as Collins was, in 1921-2, and de Valera from 1939 on). But those who grew restive were challenged in the name of the ghosts, and though survivors saw off the challenge, in their own time, the ghosts have never been exorcised. There continue to be those who say, with Pearse, they must be appeased, whatever the cost. And those who are known to be obeying the ghosts, tend to be appeased themselves, by nationalists with less impressive credentials. I shall have more to say about that.

The Crucifixion motif in *The Sovereign People* develops a sacrificial-nationalist theme, which Pearse had earlier attached, not to a mystical version of "the people" in general but to a nationalist hero. In *The Singer* – a play which, as FSL Lyons has said, "forecasts uncannily the course of his own career",[53] Pearse has his hero, MacDara, declare: "One man can free a people as one Man redeemed the world . . . I will take no pike. I will go into the battle with bare hands. I will stand up before the Gall as Christ hung naked before man on the tree."[54]

This theme had been haunting Pearse since 1913. In *The Coming Revolution* (November 1913) Pearse had offered it, with the alternative of a personal or a collective Messiah. "I do not know if the Messiah has yet come and I am not sure that there will be any visible and personal Messiah in this redemption: the people itself will perhaps be its own Messiah, the people labouring, scourged, crowned with thorns, agonising and dying, to rise again immortal and impossible."[55]

By the time Pearse came to write *The Sovereign People*, however, it would not have been seemly for him to allude even to the possibility of a personal Messiah. He was now part of a collective redemptive effort, and the hour of the redemption had been set and was about to strike. In a statement published at the end of March, 1916, the Messiah *had* to be defined collectively.

The Sovereign People was published less than a month before the Easter Rising. Pearse knew then that he could not have much more than a month to live. The very short Preface to *The Sovereign People* has a testamentary ring:

---

53. Lyons, *Ireland Since the Famine* (London, 1976), p. 337
54. *The Singer*, in P.H. Pearse, *Plays, Stories and Poems*, p. 44
55. Pearse: *Collected Works* etc p. 91

"This pamphlet concludes the examination of the Irish definition of freedom which I promised in 'Ghosts'. For my part, I have no more to say.

P.H. Pearse,
St Enda's College, Rathfarnham
1 March, 1916."

Strange as it was, Pearse's mind was original and powerful, logical and audacious, in the development of a grandiose sacrificial plan, on the basis of the premises instilled into him by his education, and inflamed into passion – no doubt fanned by personal psychic disturbances – in the emotional climate of the Home Rule crisis and the opening stages of the First World War. Pearse moved on, from the mere contemplation of Ireland as a crucified nation, to the planning of a national Resurrection and Redemption. The constitutional-nationalist support of the British war effort had been the equivalent of the Fall. The imaginative pattern is amply apparent in Pearse's writings. National Redemption combined the concepts of Crucifixion and Resurrection. Pearse would re-enact the sacrifice of Christ, within a national context. The national sacrifice would redeem the Nation (or at least the Honour of the Nation) as Christ redeemed the world. And for the symbolism to be complete, the national Crucifixion and Resurrection had to take place at Easter. The Rising was originally scheduled for Easter Sunday, but that had to be changed to Easter Monday.

Pearse was a visionary – almost in the literal sense of the word – but he was also, in his own way, a practical person, and his way resembled that of a theatrical producer. What he was aiming at essentially was the staging in Dublin of a national Passion Play, but incorporating a real life-and-death blood sacrifice. This required organisation, and the co-operation of a number of people who did not consciously share Pearse's peculiar vision, and some of whom even consciously repudiated it.

The Easter Rising was ordered, not by Pearse personally, but by a seven-member body of which Pearse was a member. This was the Military Council of the Irish Republican Brotherhood.

The Irish Republican Brotherhood was a secret and oathbound body which, on those grounds, had been under the ban of the Church since its foundation in the 1860's. Throughout the nineteenth century, and up to and including Easter 1916, the Catholic Church in Ireland was implacably opposed, at least as far as theological formulae were concerned, to revolutionary attempts. By adhering to the IRB, and then planning an insurrection which he knew to be hopeless, Pearse was doubly in mortal sin in terms of solemnly renewed spiritual instructions of the leaders of the Church of which (on his own terms) he was such a passionate devotee.

Pearse's revolutionary allies were also incongruous, ideologically speaking. They were indeed physical-force separatists, which was why Pearse was drawn to them. But their ideology, inherited from the Enlightenment and the French Revolution, put nationalism and religion into separate compartments. Theobald Wolfe Tone, universally regarded as the Father of Irish Republicanism, was as we have seen, an eighteenth-century deist, contemptuous of superstition in general and of Catholic superstition in particular. He was a secular missionary, spreading French Revolutionary ideas (in their international adaptations), hostile to Catholicism and in consequence fiercely condemned by the Church. The nationalism he preached was formally oecumenical, spurning religious differences, and seeking to unite Catholic, Protestant and Dissenter in the cause of a secular Irish Republic, hostile to Britain, and backed by Revolutionary France. Generations of Irish Republicans, inspired by the Brotherhood, had dedicated themselves to the ideals of Wolfe Tone, and so defied the authority of the Catholic Church. Curious company, one might think, for the mystical Catholic nationalist, Patrick Pearse.

The gap between Pearse and his Republican comrades was much less wide than it might appear, from the apparent contrast between his religious fervour and their secular ideology. Nationalism, however secular, or even anti-religious, in its conscious formulations, has a powerful mystique of its own. In earlier times, and in many countries, that mystique was invariably associated with religion, most notably in the case of Joan of Arc who, at the outset of her mission, announced: "He who makes war on the Holy Kingdom of France makes war on Jesus Christ." Long afterwards, in the course of the eighteenth-century Enlightenment, nationalism began to be dissociated from supernatural religion, but did not thereby lose any of its mystique. Rather the sense of exaltation and commitment, and the fanatical zeal, which had formerly adhered to religion (or to a combination of religion and nationalism incarnate in Joan of Arc) now became a cult of the nation itself. This cult predominated in the French Revolution from the very beginning, even before the fall of the Bastille. In the seminal work of the opening period of the Revolution, *What is the Third Estate?* the Abbé Sieyès declared: "The nation exists before all, it is the origin of everything. Its will is always legal, it is the law itself." The revolutionary National Assembly was founded that same year on the same principle. Later and fiercer leaders of the French Revolution made the cult more explicit and gave nationalism a monopoly of religion. A petition of the Agitators to the Legislative Assembly, in 1792, declared: "The image of the *Patrie* is the sole divinity which it is permissible to worship."[5,6]

So the worshippers of the Patrie, who were preparing the way for the French Republic, declared after the deposition of the King, late in 1792. The French Republic was of course the model for Wolfe Tone's Irish Republic, which was to inherit much of its mystique. Not through Wolfe Tone himself, during his lifetime. He was not a mystic, even a nationalist one, nor atavistically inclined. He admired the

---

56. Such quotations could easily be multiplied. Historians have generally minimised the importance of nationalism in the French Revolution. Its centrality is glaringly obvious in contemporary documents.

Revolution for sweeping away vestiges of the past – monarchy, nobility, hierarchy – not for its atavistic and millenarian overtones, which he may hardly have been aware of. The French Directory, with which he had to deal from 1796, was itself drifting away from the Republic, through corruption, towards military rule. The Irish revolutionaries who responded to the mystical-millenarian *potential* of the French Revolution were not Wolfe Tone's friends, but those whom his friends were to accept as unexpected and disturbing but indispensable allies: the Defenders. As we have seen, these saw the French Revolutionaries as Catholic liberators, the Chief Consul arm-in-arm with Simon Peter. The actual relation of religion and the French Revolution to the Irish rebellion of 1798 was complex and full of ironies. But in Pearsean retrospect, it all became simple. The Defenders disappeared from view; it was all Wolfe Tone and the United Irishmen, but a version of those that had far more in common than Tone and his friends originally had, with the Defender tradition of mystical Catholic nationalism.

That mystique, lingering but apparently fading in the late-nineteenth and early twentieth century, flared up apocalyptically after the sacrificial Proclamation of the Republic on Easter Monday, 1916. The opening words of the Proclamation are throughly Pearsean, with a Yeatsian influence:

"Irishmen and Irishwomen: In the name of God and of the dead generations from which she receives her old tradition of nationhood, Ireland, through us, summons her children to her flag and strikes for her freedom."

In one of the pamphlets written amid the preparations for the Rising – *The Spiritual Nation* (February, 1916) – Pearse had written about a personified Ireland, and about that play of Yeats's:

"When I was a child I believed that there was actually a woman called Erin and had Mr. Yeats's Kathleen ni Houlihan been then written and had I seen it, I should have taken it, not as an allegory, but as a representation of a thing that might happen any day in any house".[57]

The personified "Ireland" of the Proclamation, the mother who summons her children to come out and be killed, is identical with the Old Woman of Yeats's *Cathleen ni Houlihan*. And she goes back a long way beyond that into the folk memory.

The executions which followed the Proclamation sealed that document in blood and made it a sacral document for generations of Irish nationalists.

In the preparation of those events, Pearse's personal mysticism had played the leading part, but it had struck a responsive chord in the hearts of Republicans whose rhetoric had been secular, but whose emotional tradition went back to an older world. Pearse's mysticism drew them to him through the glowing intensity which it imparted to his personality, oratory and writings. A mystique which was to be immensely intensified after the sacrificial Proclamation of the Republic on Easter Monday 1916. Even before that, it is clear that Irish Republicans were already deeply attracted by the Pearsean mystique, however remote it might seem from the formally secular aspects of the Republican tradition. Pearse's mystical fervour in no way put them off, strange though it was to the conscious part of their tradition. The socialist, James Connolly, had earlier sneered at Pearse's sacramental exaltation of "the red wine of the battlefield." But by 1916 Connolly is talking in exactly the same vein, as if he had been mesmerised by Pearse. Pearse had power over Connolly because of the superior intensity and singlemindedness of his nationalism; the intensity being derived from the fusion of nationalism with religion. Before the outbreak of the First World War, Pearse was already an exalted nationalist, while Connolly still thought of himself as a socialist, first and foremost. Pearse had been dismissive about that sort of thing: "I am nothing so

---

57. Pearse, *Collected Works* etc. pp. 300-301

new-fangled as a socialist or syndicalist. I am old-fashioned enough to be both a Catholic and a nationalist," he wrote in October, 1913.[58]

From the outbreak of war on, Connolly is becoming more and more "old-fashioned" and less and less "newfangled". He is getting acquainted with ghosts. By February 1916, with the Rising now determined, Connolly has completely capitulated to Pearse. Connolly writes:

"But deep in the heart of Ireland has sunk the sense of the degradation wrought upon its people – a degradation so deep and so humiliating that no agency less powerful than the red tide of war in Irish soil will ever be able to enable (sic) the Irish race to recover its self-respect . . . Without the slightest trace of irreverence but in all humility and awe, we recognize that of us, as of mankind before Calvary it may truly be said, 'without the shedding of Blood there is no Redemption."[58a]

In a sense, Connolly was falling under Pearse's spell, but in a wider sense both are under the same spell, in the period from 1914 to 1916.

Both Pearse and Connolly were under the spell of a mystical nationalism which goes back at least to the vision-poems of the late Middle Ages, in which France, Germany, Ireland and other countries had been personified and virtually deified, within an exalted poetic imagery fusing religion and nationalism. In most of Europe, by the nineteenth century, this was an archaic literary form, but in Ireland the vision-poem – *Aisling* – was a living force in the Gaelic tradition and close to the heart of Patrick Pearse, himself a gifted Gaelic poet, though in an Edwardian vein. The nearer you get to mediaeval Christianity the nearer you get to the pagan world, and early twentieth-century Ireland was closer to mediaeval Christianity than most of Europe was. (And it is still closer than it is consciously aware of.)

Pearse and Connolly had been receiving their ancestral voices through somewhat differing channels and with

---

58. Quoted in Lyons, *Ireland since the Famine*, p. 333
58a. Quoted in C Desmond Greaves *The Life and Times of James Connolly*, pp. 318-319

different echoes. For Pearse, the channel and the echoes, through which the nationalistic mystique was conveyed, were mainly Catholic and sacramental, around the concept of "crucified nation". For Connolly the channel and the echoes were Republican rather than Catholic but from a Republican tradition which was ultimately mystical and nationalist with a secular overlay. But it was an imaginative field in which distinctions were less important than a common exaltation: Cathleen ni Houlihan was summoning the elect among her children. [59] The summons came out of a world older than Catholicism, let alone the French Revolution. As Yeats expressed it, with remarkable insight:

"When Pearse summoned Cuchulainn to his side
What stalked through the Post Office?"

But the summons, ancient as was the emotional power behind it, had to be expressed in a modern political idiom capable of challenging contemporary political formulae based on expediency and prudence. In that area, Pearse had to defer, formally, to Connolly and other Republicans. You do not send out a manifesto asking people to join you in a crucifixion.

So the formula of the Republic imposed itself. It had the advantage of being uncompromisingly political, yet with mystical overtones. It was not negotiable, since it negated the Crown, the symbol of the rejected alien mystique. Its credentials, in terms of the nationalist mystique, were insurpassable. It was to the cause of the Republic – Tone's Republic supported by the French Republic, One and Indivisible – that Cathleen ni Houlihan had summoned the elect among her children in 1798. The second summons was that of 1916.

The Republic proclaimed in 1916, having been sealed by the blood-sacrifice, transcended its limited, literal institutional-political meaning, and acquired sacral status. The sacral Republic would not be achieved, in literal actuality here below, in 1916, as the signatories to the Proclamation well knew. But the Proclamation was not only the signal for an immediate once-off blood-sacrifice, claiming all its signatories

---

59. *Yeats*'s Cathleen ni Houlihan, a pedant might say. But Cathleen was a force, quite independent of Yeats. In Irish Republican terms, Yeats had become a drop-out, or sell-out, long before 1916 (since 1903 in fact, the year after that play). But the creature he no longer cared for had a life of her own, like Frankenstein's artifact.

and many others. It was also a blessing on an indefinite number of further blood-sacrifices, in order to attain a kind of sacral-political Second Coming: the ultimate terrestrial advent of the Republic proclaimed at Easter 1916.

Pearsean Republicanism was a Catholic affair and, like Catholicism, detached from, and immune to democratic values. The seven signatories of the Proclamation were all Catholics. James Connolly had probably been an agnostic, but like many an Irish-Catholic agnostic, he died a good Catholic. He received the last sacraments immediately before his execution. This fact was widely reported, and seems to have been a significant factor in the general retrospective adoption of the Rising by Catholic Ireland, albeit in a diluted and confused version of the sacral character imputed to the Rising by the signatories of the Proclamation. The ecclesiastically-correct circumstances of Connolly's death confirmed, at the level of popular emotions, the nature of the Rising as the most exalted expression of Irish Catholic nationalism.

That was how it worked at the level of popular emotions. But at an intellectual level, where rational distinctions are perceptible, there were basic cognitive difficulties. Republicanism had come to mean two incompatible things. There was Tone's Republicanism, and there was Pearse's Republicanism. Tone's Republicanism was oecumenical, in terms of religious affiliation, embracing Catholics, Protestants and Dissenters. Pearse's Republicanism grew out of the Catholic nationalism he was taught by the Christian Brothers, and is an exalted and mystical version of the same. Pearse pays extravagant homage to Tone, but the Tone he admires is a creation of his own: a Catholicised and mysticized Tone. As an ideology, "the Republicanism of Tone and Pearse" is a mass of contradictions. But as a cult, something to be practised without question, Pearsian Republicanism (incorporating sacralised Tone) is formidable indeed. It is a sensitive medium for hearing voices and seeing ghosts; and what the voices and the ghosts are calling for is blood. Calling for it and getting it, in the Ireland of the late twentieth century.

115

Most people in Catholic and nationalist Ireland, after 1921, came to regard themselves as Republicans. The largest party in the Republic of Ireland (not Pearse's Republic, the Twenty-Six County one) is the Republican Party, aka Fianna Fáil. Many in the other parties also call themselves Republicans. All the dominant rhetoric of the culture was Republican.

Generations of Irish Catholic politicians were to speak of "the need to rededicate ourselves to the ideals of 1916". The cult has not been, for most of the people, as the twentieth century wore on, something fervently and passionately held, but rather something hesitant and mostly subliminal, tinged with apprehension and with guilt. De Valera's words, spoken immediately after the surrender of the garrison at Boland's Mills were troubling: "if the people had only come out, even with knives and forks . . . " They came out only retrospectively, with uneasy homage.

Uneasy as it is, and increasingly so, the homage has been remarkably durable, and has had far-reaching political implications, which are taking increasingly disturbing forms in the late twentieth century.

Here we need to take account of that differential. There are Republicans and Republicans. There are mild ones, and there are fierce ones. The milder variety is much the more numerous; specimens of it populate the Dáil and Senate of the Republic. The fierce variety is fairly common in Northern Ireland, very rare in the Republic. Both varieties are aware of the ghosts but behave differently with regard to them. The mild Republicans propitiate the ghosts, on public occasions, but privately hope they will soon be laid to rest, or at least keep fairly quiet. The raison d'etre of the fierce variety is to obey the Pearsean imperative: "You must do the thing it asks you." Meaning: to provide it with blood.

Now within the Republican culture, the person who is doing the thing the ghost asks has a clear moral ascendancy over the person who is, as it were, dodging the ghost's eye. There is a notable contemporary example of this ascendancy; I shall be discussing this towards the end of this book.

In the political statements of Sinn Féin-IRA, there is seldom any trace of Pearsean rhetoric. It is only when you watch the funerals that you get the message. The milder Republicans are uncomfortable with Pearse, and in consequence respectfully vague. But the fiercer sort is interested in what might be called the animist streak in Pearsean Republicanism: the ghosts and the graves. And it derives its standing licence to kill from Pearse's speech at the grave of O'Donovan Rossa: ". . . and while Ireland holds these graves, Ireland unfree shall never be at peace."[60]

THE HIERARCHY AND THE CULT OF 1916

Pearse's vision was retrospectively validated, in an ambiguous sort of way, as a result of the martyrdom he had deliberately sought. The Rising was unpopular in Ireland when it happened. Scores of thousands of Catholic Irish were fighting in British uniforms at the time, against those whom the Proclamation of the Republic referred to as "gallant allies in Europe". The dependants of the soldiers reacted against the Rising initially, as a stab in the back to their men. But the executions that followed the Rising produced a great revulsion. Yeats's "terrible beauty" was born as a result of the executions, not of the Rising. As the executions were spun out, over a period of weeks, Irish history, as taught by the Christian Brothers, seemed to be coming to life, in the twentieth century. The support which Irish nationalists had given to the British war-effort in 1914 came to appear repugnant and almost incredible, when looked back upon in the atmosphere of the summer of 1916. Soon, a cult of the martyrs of 1916 was under way, and began to be exploited politically, with the release of the survivors of the Rising in 1917.

In terms of the subject of the present essay, the phenomenon of greatest interest at this point in the story is the

---

60. O'Donovan Rossa, graveside oration, August 1915: *Collected Works* etc pp. 133 – 138

accommodation reached in 1917-18, between the Catholic Church and the Cult of 1916. This was a tricky passage for the Church leaders to negotiate, both theologically and politically. In terms of Catholic theology, as taught in the nineteenth and twentieth century, both in Ireland and elsewhere, the Rising of 1916 was doubly sinful: in that it had had no hope of success (at least once it was clear that German help was not coming) and it had been ordered and led by members of a secret and oathbound society. In addition, Pearse's mystical fusion of religion and Irish nationalism was clearly heretical and his elevation of Wolfe Tone above St Patrick was offensive to pious ears, not to mention his doubts as to whether the Messiah had arrived. Pearse's cult of Cuchulain and his tendency to mingle in imagination the pagan warrior's death with the Passion of Jesus Christ, suggested a disquieting mixture of paganism with modern decadence. Nor was there anything Christian about Cathleen ni Houlihan. The whole climate of the Rising was unattractive, at least to the conscious minds of orthodox and conventional Catholics.

On the other hand, there were political reasons for turning a blind eye to the peculiar theological and psychological aspects of the Rising. The Church, as we have seen, as well as supporting constitutional nationalism, had also enouraged a fiercely Anglophobic form of religious nationalism, and many, probably most, of those who took part in the Rising were religious nationalists of precisely the type which the Church had encouraged. The Church had not intended that the nationalism which it encouraged should lead to revolution. The Christian Brothers were instructed to discourage their pupils from violent applications of the patriotic zeal which had been inculcated in them. (That is why Brother Craven, Pearse's teacher, was regarded as exceptional). Cardinal Cullen and his colleagues had neither desired revolution nor thought it at all probable. But what they were ensuring – consciously or not – was that if there *were* a revolution, it should be a *Catholic* revolution. And this was what was happening, beginning with the Rising of 1916. True, the

Catholics concerned were a bit heterodox, but that had to be expected, granted the tensions between the religious nationalism which the Church had encouraged, and the Church's condemnation of revolution and revolutionary preparations.

There were also practical reasons deterring the Irish Hierarchy from denouncing the Cult of 1916. Sinn Féin, the party founded by Eamon de Valera,[61] the senior surviving Commandant of 1916, was rising in popularity, and the constitutional nationalists were in decline. This was only partly due to the "terrible beauty" factor. Throughout Europe, by 1917, there was a vast disillusion with the war-effort, in proportion to the slaughter which had resulted from it. In Ireland, this revulsion – combining with resistance to a British attempt to impose conscription in the Spring of 1918 – favoured Sinn Féin as against the Irish Parliamentary Party, which had supported the war-effort. Sinn Féin was treating the elections which would follow the war's end as a kind of retrospective vote of confidence in the Easter Rising. This was tricky for the Church, theologically, and also dangerous, since it seemed to point to further hostilities. On the other hand it could be dangerous, for the Church itself, to confront Sinn Féin. The Church had had confrontations with nationalist forces before – most recently in 1890-1891, over the Parnell divorce case – and though it had won, its authority had been somewhat impaired for a time, especially in Dublin and among the young. And Sinn Féin, in 1917-18, looked incomparably stronger than the (post-Divorce) Parnellites had ever looked.

In the circumstances, it was no doubt inevitable that a deal should be done, and it was, without fanfare, in the run up to the 1918 elections, between de Valera and the most politic member of the Hierarchy, Archbishop Walsh, a worthy heir to the politic Paul Cullen. The terms of the deal were never announced, and they can only be inferred from the sequel.

---

61. Technically, he did not found it, but took over and gave a different direction to, an older party of the same name: Arthur Griffith's Sinn Féin, which had not been in the physical force tradition. Griffith acquiesced in the take-over.

Individual churchmen, here and there, grumbled about Sinn Féin, but the Church as a collectivity took no position, which was equivalent to leaving the Irish Parliamentary Party to its fate: twisting slowly in the wind. The *quid pro quo* was that education would be left under the control of the Catholic Hierarchy, where British law had placed it. Archbishop Walsh let it be known that he had voted for Sinn Féin. The public announcement came only after the election, but it cannot have come as a surprise to the clergy of Walsh's diocese.

In the elections of November 1918, Sinn Féin won almost all the popularly-elected seats in Catholic Ireland: Eastern Ulster voted unionist. The elected Sinn Féiners, as promised, refused to take their seats in the Parliament of the United Kingdom. They met as the Parliament of Ireland, Dáil Eireann, and elected a Government, in competition with the British one. They set up Government Departments, paralleling the existing United Kingdom ones, in every sphere of Government with one exception, Education. There was no Minister for Education, under the First Dáil. No reason was ever supplied for this omission but the reason is obvious. The revolution was to leave the Church untouched. It would carry on its educational business as usual throughout the troubles. A tacit concordat was being honoured.[62]

Sinn Féin had fought the elections on a platform that did not sound revolutionary; they would withdraw from the British Parliament and appeal to the Peace Conference, on the basis of Wilson's Fourteen Points. It was inherently improbable that a Conference dominated by the victorious Allied and Associated Powers would listen to a Party which proudly claimed descent from rebels who, during the World War, had hailed the Central Powers as their gallant allies in Europe. But the people were led to believe that Sinn Féin could achieve this peaceful outcome.

---

62. See David W Miller, *Church, State and Nation in Ireland 1898-1921* (Dublin 1983) pp. 440-1. When the question was raised in the Dáil in 1920, Cathal Brugha, (standing in for President de Valera, then in America), "replied that he thought President de Valera had some definite reason for not appointing a Minister for Education . . . " The whole Dáil would have understood what that meant.

What the people actually got was two-and-a-half years of guerrilla war, with the usual atrocities on both sides. Neither Church nor people had bargained for this. The Church condemned the violence, on both sides, but with more emphasis on British acts of repression than on Irish acts of rebellion. When the eventual compromise came, with the Anglo-Irish Treaty of 1921, Sinn Féin split and the Church threw its full weight behind the pro-Treaty forces in the subsequent Civil War. The anti-Treaty side called itself the Republican side and claimed to be defending the ideals of 1916 against those who had betrayed them. This claim was rejected, but would have been difficult to refute. The Church excommunicated the anti-Treaty leaders, whose forces were defeated in a five-months civil war.

The Church, by this time, had had enough of the exalted religious nationalism, which it had encouraged (while attempting to set limits to it) in the nineteenth century, and connived at from 1916 to 1919. But Catholic bishops are not in the habit of acknowledging their own errors, and instead of acknowledging this one, they compounded it. In 1917-18, they had condoned the cult of 1916, for the most part tacitly. Now they associated themselves with it. Neither they, nor the new Government which they had helped to instal, could afford not to contest the formidable title deeds which the Republican side possessed, to being the heirs of 1916. Both sides claimed to be the heirs in question. One side encouraged the cult of the Rising, the other could not afford to discourage it. Ornate copies of the Proclamation became part of the iconography of the culture, in association with emblems of more traditional religion, such as crucifixes. In the haunted realms of symbolism, Pearse's ideals were indeed being achieved.

Now, if the Republic proclaimed by Pearse and Connolly and their comrades had in fact come into being, there would be no harm in a cult of the Founders or their Proclamation. It could be a factor of stability, like the cult of Washington and Jefferson, within the civic religion of the United States. But as that Republic did not come into being, the cult of its Proclamation, within a State which is less than that proclaimed, is profoundly unsettling, for the generations of children who have been exposed to it, and for the adults they became.

Among those who don't take it all that seriously, it is conducive to hypocrisy, or to cynicism, or to a kind of frivolous insouciance about the meaning of words and concepts. Among the minority who take it altogether seriously, it is the standing symbol that sanctions political violence, and contempt for the State (and Church) that pay lip-service to the symbol. And there are many – perhaps even a majority – who, while not taking the Proclamation altogether seriously, feel a bit guilty about this, and a bit in awe of those who do take it seriously, and act on it.

HANNA AND SEAN

An ominous feature for the new State was the intensity with which the cult of 1916 was still adhered to by a significant minority, in the aftermath of the Irish civil war. My aunt, Hanna Sheehy-Skeffington, was one of the most ardent and implacable guardians of the sacred flame. In an autobiographical excerpt published in *The Atlantic Monthly* in January, 1994 I give an account of an encounter between Hanna and Sean O'Casey:

"Hanna Sheehy-Skeffington took part in the protests that turned into a riot on the fourth night of Sean O'Casey's *The Plough and the Stars* in the Abbey Theatre, Dublin. On the first night of *Plough*, 8 February, 1926, WB Yeats, the directing spirit of the Abbey Theatre since its foundation, made the occasion something of a political demonstration. This was less than three years after the end of the Irish Civil War. Yeats was a member of the Senate of the Irish Free State, having been nominated to it by the victors in the civil war, and he invited some of the luminaries of the Free State government to the performance and dinner. Gabriel Fallon, a close friend of O'Casey's, suggested that Yeats hoped the play would 'score over his Republican enemies'. This was an understatement. Yeats knew that the play would drive the Republicans almost out of their minds. They would see it as both the hijacking and the defilement of the 1916 rising, by the poet-senator who had betrayed its ideals. In the conditions of post-civil-war Dublin, violent protests were certain. Yeats had no objection to that. He enjoyed real-life theatre, with the Abbey at the centre of the excitement. O'Casey, on the other hand (a little like Salman Rushdie later), seems to have had no idea of the fires he was kindling.

The first night, with a safe Free State audience, passed off without incident. As Hanna's biographers tell the story: 'On the second night, there were some audience objections when the Republican flag was brought into the pub in Act 11 and on the third night these protests were even more pronounced and seemed to be directed at the young prostitute.' Gabriel Fallon is described as having seen the protesters 'as divided into two groups: those, like Hanna, who objected on nationalistic grounds and others who found the play morally offensive.' This is rather too neat, and too cerebral. The whole protest was *both* nationalistic *and* religious. For Irish Republicans the Easter Rising was (and still is, for those who are killing in its name) a sacred event – as Pearse intended it to be, timing it accordingly. *The Plough and the Stars* was felt as a desecration. Both the pub and the prostitute were part of the desecration, which occurs when the Republican flag is brought into the pub and when Pearse's voice is heard proclaiming the Republic in that unhallowed context.

The second and third nights of *Plough* were the warm-up. The big night was the fourth, Thursday, Hanna's night. Eamon de Valera – then seen as the heir of Pearse and Connolly – had appointed Hanna director of organisation of Sinn Féin, and I have no doubt that she organised the Thursday-night demonstration. Her biographers write:

'All accounts agree that on Thursday night disapproval climaxed in a Republican demonstration: all seem to agree that Hanna led it . . . During the second act she arose and shouted that the play was "traducing the men of 1916". From that point on nobody could hear the dialogue on stage and minor battles were breaking out in various parts of the threatre. Through it all, Hanna continued to orate. [Hanna's feminist biographers are uncomfortable with her passionate nationalism – C.C.O'B.] Before the fourth act began, Yeats brought in the police and the hall was cleared of protestors. Hanna, leaving the theatre under police escort, made one last dramatic speech. "I am one of the widows of Easter Week," she said. "It is no wonder that you do not remember the men of Easter Week, because none of you fought on either side.'"

In Hanna's mind Frank had joined the sixteen executed leaders of the rising. And in spirit he did indeed belong with them.

The controversy continued in print, in *The Irish Independent*, between Hanna and O'Casey. There was one sentence in the exchange which I read with another of those shivers, when I came across it recently in Hanna's biography. Referring to the spirit of 1916 she wrote, 'That Mr. O'Casey is blind to it does not necessarily prove that it is non-existent, but merely that his vision is defective.'

O'Casey's vision already *was* defective, in the literal sense, and he was threatened with blindness. Hanna, being a civilised person, would never have deliberately alluded to a physical defect of any opponent. But the demon of nationalism, which had her in its grip, selected, through her unconscious mind, the metaphor that would hit the enemy at his weakest point.

At the end of the same letter, she took a swipe at Yeats: 'For they shall be remembered for ever by the people if not by the Abbey directorate.'

This was an allusion to the punch line of Cathleen ni Houlihan, which Yeats had written at a time when he, like Hanna now, was in the grip of manic nationalism (in his case, that of Maud Gonne, Hanna's friend and ally). Still, considering the heat of the circumstances, she dealt gently enough with Yeats, whose poetry she admired. She knew about good writing, and could appreciate it even coming from an ideological enemy. I owe a lifelong debt to her for that characteristic, for it was she who first introduced me to good writing, through the works of that great British imperialist Rudyard Kipling. She gave me *The Jungle Book* for my ninth birthday. That was near the end of the year of *The Plough and the Stars.*

The climax of the controversy took the form of a public debate between Hanna and O'Casey, which of course Hanna won hands down. Her biographers wrote:

'When O'Casey's turn came, he had to face an already hostile audience. His vision was bad, his glasses blurred, and he had great difficulty deciphering his notes. After struggling for some five minutes, he said that he could not go on and sat down. Hanna sympathised, sensing that, had he been an experienced public speaker like herself, he would have "had a lot more to say".'

Possibly, as she watched O'Casey's performance, Hanna experienced some remorse for that metaphor of hers. Shortly after that grisly encounter, O'Casey left Ireland for good. Having experienced, on more than one occasion over the years, brief touches of my aunt Hanna's cold and measured wrath, I can well understand O'Casey's flight, after bearing the brunt of her all-out attack."

Thus far my autobiographical account. But there is another dimension to that encounter, which I ignored in that account, but which comes to life for me, in the context of my present theme. Sean O'Casey was a Protestant. Furthermore, he was a Protestant belonging to a category held in peculiar abhorrence and contempt by Irish Catholics well into the present century. He was a working-class Protestant. Working-class Protestants were generally assumed to belong to families which had originally been Catholic but had been suborned by proselytisers, with money or food. These were popularly known as "soupers", the soup distributed by proselytisers in famine times to people willing to change their religion. The whole audience at that public debate had to be acutely aware of that dimension, accentuating their hostility to the blasphemer against 1916, justifying that nationalist hostility in traditional Catholic terms, and edging it with righteous contempt.

MICHAEL COLLINS'S NORTHERN WAR

The cult of 1916 was never abandoned and its power continued to be felt. Yet in the daylight world of practical political arrangements, from 1921-22 on, the Republic proclaimed in 1916 was being laid aside, or so it seemed, in favour of the Irish Free State, a product of pragmatic compromise. For the pro-Treaty side, especially those who had fought for the Republic, and now had formed the Government of the Free State, this was an enormously difficult transition. Their adversaries represented all the power (temporarily shrunken though it might be) of the old mystique. It is true that by 1922-3, just after the grim experience of "the Troubles" of 1919-21, most Irish people were heartily tired of Cathleen ni Houlihan and all that she had landed them into. The Treaty side won a clear victory in free elections in 1922 (in the territory allocated to the Free State). That territory consisted of Twenty-six counties. The Six Counties of the North-East were now (since 1920) a partly-autonomous province (Northern Ireland) within the United Kingdom of Great Britain and Northern Ireland. What Northern Ireland represented was a secession from a secession.The almost homogenously Catholic part of Ireland was seceding from the United Kingdom, but the Ulster Protestants (a majority in Eastern Ulster) refused to follow that secession. Northern Ireland was now divided into two political entities, one of them almost homogenously Catholic and the other Protestant-majority.

Those who voted for the pro-Treaty candidates in the elections of 1922 were accepting at least the *de facto* existence of Northern Ireland. Or were they? The leading figure on the pro-Treaty side, Michael Collins, was not. Michael Collins was the best-known leader of the rebel side in the 1919-21 period, and he was now by far the most popular figure on the side of the Treaty, which he had helped to negotiate. His adversaries in Ireland charged him with abandoning the Republic which he had sworn to serve, and the charge was highly plausible in the circumstances. It was also difficult for him to deny the charge, explicitly, since his British partners, in concluding the Treaty, regarded the Irish side as settling for something well short of a Republic, which was indeed literally the case. But what we are talking about is usually not the domain of the literal.

Collins's formula, which became basic to the pro-Treaty side, was that the Treaty gave "freedom to achieve freedom". This was generally regarded as expressive of a determination to improve on the Treaty, from a nationalist point of view, gradually, through a process of negotiation. This was a tolerable position, for the British side, and it was also congenial to the Irish electorate, sick of violence. But there was a concealed agenda, within the "freedom to achieve freedom". Collins, in the period immediately after the Treaty, gave covert Free State support to guerrilla operations in Northern Ireland.[63]

In nationalist terms this represented the defence of "our people" against Orange (ie Protestant) aggression. The Protestant side, of course, thought they were defending themselves against Catholic aggression. In fact, each side went on the offensive whenever it could, and on the defensive whenever it had to. It was a brutal sectarian-political war over contested turf. What was remarkable was that a Government, founded on an agreement with Britain, was covertly contributing to a war against the Protestants in Northern Ireland. The assassination in 1922 of Sir Henry Wilson, former Chief of the Imperial Staff, was part of that war. Wilson was an Irish Protestant (born in Co Longford) and an ardent political champion of the Ulster unionists. It seems to have been Collins who ordered Wilson's assassination.

---

63. See Tim Pat Coogan, *Michael Collins: a Biography* (London, 1991)

This application of "freedom to achieve freedom" had Northern Ireland as its target. But the wider political aim was to reunite nationalist Catholics – bitterly divided over the Treaty – under the sign of a common and ancient hostility to the Ulster Protestants. Collins stuck to this strategy, as far as he could, but Republican diehards could not forgive him the Treaty. After he was shot by one of these, in the summer of 1922, his successor WT Cosgrave called off the covert hostilities against Northern Ireland, and concentrated on finishing off the civil war in the South. Later, in 1925, the same Free State Government recognised the existing borders of Northern Ireland in order to avert the danger that the borders might be revised to the detriment of the Free State.

The period of Collins's covert war against Northern Ireland was a brief one – no more than six months. But the pattern of thinking and feeling behind it is abiding and has come to the surface since, from time to time, in 1969 for example and again in 1993-4. It is something which nationalist politicians have drawn on, in different degrees in different circumstances. There has always been a good deal of ambivalence around, and Northern Ireland has been a kind of joker in the pack of Catholic-nationalist ambivalence. On the one hand, one wants peace with it; on the other hand, one wants to destroy it. And there is an underlying synthesis, in many minds; peace will be achieved, eventually, through the destruction of Northern Ireland.

DE VALERA'S FLAWED COMEBACK

The most important nationalist leaders of the twentieth century, Michael Collins and Eamon de Valera, both rang the changes on that ambivalence. Collins signed a Treaty, setting up a Free State which did not include Northern Ireland, and then used the resources of the Free State, in an effort to subvert Northern Ireland. De Valera originally – during the Treaty debates – accepted the legitimacy of partition, in principle. He argued that any county which did not want to be included in the Republic had a right to opt out. "Document No. 2" – de Valera's alternative to the Treaty – embodied that principle, as regards Northern Ireland.

Northern Ireland was not, therefore, de Valera's reason for throwing his weight against the Treaty, and in favour of the Republican (or "irregular") side in the civil war. (Analysis of his reasons, which remain debatable, would take us out of the confines of the present study). But after the defeat of the Republicans, and after the recognition of the borders of Northern Ireland by the Free State, de Valera, in a fiery speech in 1925, denied any legitimacy to Northern Ireland and called the recognition of its borders a betrayal. He declared, on 10 December, 1925: "For Republicans there can be no two opinions on that question. We may have to bow our heads for a time to the enforced partition of our country by a foreign Power, but the sanction of our consent that partition can never have.

"We deny that any part of our people can give away the sovereignty or alienate any part of this nation or territory. If this generation should be base enough to consent to give them away, the right to win them back remains unimpaired for those to whom the future will bring the opportunity."

Whatever de Valera's motives in making this move, it was tactically rewarding, through its powerful appeal to Catholic nationalism.

Most Irish Catholics, in the mid-1920's, did not want to reopen the whole question of the Treaty, with that topic's inherent tendency to re-ignite the war. Nor was there any electoral mileage whatever in de Valera's actual alternative to the Treaty, Document No. 2, which was so like the Treaty itself as to be embarrassing in retrospect. On the other hand, a carefully-limited challenge to the Government over conceding *in a post-Treaty document*, more to the Protestants of Northern Ireland than even the Treaty conceded to them, had great pan-Catholic-nationalist potential. By this move, with its subliminal acquiescence in the *fait accompli* of the Treaty itself, de Valera was broadening his political constituency, bringing himself towards the centre of the Catholic-nationalist UMMA. This politic and potent transaction helped to prepare the way for de Valera's emergence as victor in the general elections of 1932. The coming to power of the person regarded (not quite accurately) as the great loser in the civil war of 1922, through free and fair elections ten years later, was a remarkable happening, and considerably to the credit of both sides.

The change was generally regarded as stabilising democracy in what is now the Republic of Ireland (Twenty-Six Counties). There was much truth in that, but there was also a flaw in the achievement. De Valera's achievement was partly based on the appeal to Catholic-nationalist passions that was contained in his denunciation of the recognition of Northern Ireland's borders. In office, de Valera gave constitutional effect among the Catholic population, to the denial of Northern Ireland's legitimacy. But the claim to Northern Ireland remained inert during all the years when de Valera was in office. As he said on 1 March, 1933, near the beginning of his long, first period of office: " The only policy for abolishing partition that I can see is for us, in this part of Ireland to use such freedom as we can secure to get for the people in this part of Ireland such conditions as will make the people in the other part of Ireland wish to belong to this part".

During the Second World War, when de Valera had declared neutrality, he assured the British that Ireland (as the former Free State now officially described itself) would not allow its territory to be used as a basis for attack on Britain. Not only was he as good as his word but he included Northern Ireland (*de facto*) in that guarantee. De Valera ruthlessly crushed the attempts of the post-Treaty IRA to act on Tone's doctrine, which was also Pearse's doctrine, "England's difficulty is Ireland's opportunity". The IRA's position, in terms of the Republican ideology, was impeccable and in no way impaired by the IRA's status as a small minority. But the senior surviving officer of the 1916 Rising was unimpressed by these ideological credentials. He interned IRA personnel and close sympathisers. He allowed those on hunger-strike to die, and he sanctioned the execution of those who were convicted of murder.

SON OF MAUD GONNE

By 1948, the de Valera Government had been in power for sixteen consecutive years. Among those who felt it was time for a change were the IRA, aka "the Republican Movement". These were not in a position, on their own, to mount an electoral challenge to the Government, even through their recognised political arm, Sinn Féin. But the IRA badly needed to get de Valera out, not only in order to avenge what he had done to them during the war years, but also to acquire greater security for the rebuilding of their organisation and the eventual resumption of their operations. They needed a new party, with a chance of getting elected in sufficient strength to be represented in a coalition government, and which would be certain not to acquiesce in severe measures (such as internment) against the IRA. They found such a party in the newly-founded Clann na Poblachta (children of the Republic), founded and led by Sean MacBride, a personality in whom they rightly felt they could have full confidence, in those matters which concerned them most. His party's name met their specifications. It implied that this party and not de Valera's Fianna Fáil (which styled itself, in English, the Republican Party) were the true heirs of the Republic proclaimed in 1916.

Sean MacBride was the son of Maud Gonne and Major John MacBride. Sean was born in Paris (in January, 1904), but his mother brought him to Ireland to be baptised. (John O'Leary was to be the godfather, but the priest refused to let him, because O'Leary was a known Fenian). Maud and her children then returned to France, where Sean was brought up. Maud did not want to bring Sean back to Ireland in case MacBride laid claim to him.[64] The break-up of the MacBride

---

64. *Gonne-Yeats Letters*, Introduction, p. 32

marriage began in October, 1904, when Sean was less than a year old. The separation was complete, after an appeal, by January 1908. Maud wrote to Yeats: . . . "The monthly visits which Seagan [Sean] was to have paid to his father each year when he was six years old have been suppressed and the visits which MacBride, by the first verdict, had a right to receive twice a week have been reduced to once a week but my request that they should take place at my house or at the house of the doctor has been refused. This is very great cause for upset and anxiety for it facilitates MacBride stealing the child and I shall have great worry and expense making things quite safe. However for the last 18 months MacBride has not once asked to see the child and as he is not likely to live in Paris I hope these visits will be a dead letter. Still they are always a nuisance and will prevent me living in Ireland for the present".[65]

There is a portrait of Sean, by his mother, done in the same year in which that letter was written.[66] It is an arresting and disturbing portrait. The child's expression is not that of a child but of an ageless being: tense and brooding and apparently confronting dark forces. Sean's arms are folded on his chest.

In the context of that letter, written in the same year, this looks to me like the picture of a little boy who has been told he is in danger of being kidnapped by his wicked father.

Maud's anxiety that John MacBride might somehow get hold of Sean continued up to as late as 1915, when Sean was eleven.[67] But then came 1916: Major John MacBride was executed on May 5.

On May 11, Maud wrote to Yeats: "Major MacBride by his Death has left a name for Seagan [Sean] to be proud of. Those who die for Ireland are sacred".[68] Later, speaking of all the executed leaders she quoted *Cathleen ni Houlihan*: "The deaths of those leaders are full of beauty and romance. They

---

65. Gonne to Yeats (January 1908). *Gonne-Yeats Letters*, p. 253
66. The portrait is reproduced in the *Gonne-Yeats Letters* facing p. 220
67. *Gonne-Yeats Letters*, pp. 352-4, letters of December, 1914 and January 1915.
68. *Gonne-Yeats Letters* p. 377

will be speaking for ever, the people shall hear them for ever."[69]

For Sean, then aged twelve, the birth of Yeats's "terrible beauty" must have been especially wrenching and poignant. The father whom he had never known, and towards whom he must have entertained feelings of aversion and apprehension (at best) was now metamorphosed into a sacred being in the eyes of his mother, who had loathed his father, for as long as Sean's memories could go back. Yet he must have instantly recognised the legitimacy of the totally unexpected metamorphosis for he had been brought up, by his mother, on a peculiarly intense mystical-nationalist form of the cult of those who died for Ireland.

In November, 1915 – five months before the Easter Rising – Maud Gonne wrote to Yeats of a vision she had had about "the Souls of the Dead". She had seen the spirits of Irish soldiers killed in the World War, and of these she writes with respect and sympathy, but not with any reverence, and then she goes on to those who died for Ireland:

"Others have died with a definite idea of sacrifice to an ideal, they were held by the stronger and deeper rhythms of the chants, leading in wonderful patterns to a deeper peace, the peace of the Crucified, which is above the currents of nationalities and storms, but for all that they will not be separated from Ireland for as an entity she has followed the path of Sacrifice and has tasted of the Grail and the strength they will bring her is greater.[70]

Maud saw that vision a little over a month before Pearse delivered his message of Christmas Day, 1915, about "the power of the ghosts of a nation". Sean MacBride was brought up under that power, and it had to be strengthened by the addition of his formerly alienated father to the number of the ghosts in question.

In 1918, Maud Gonne and her son returned to Ireland. Maud was jailed for subversive activities, and Sean joined the

---

69. *Gonne-Yeats Letters*, p. 395
70. *Gonne-Yeats Letters*, p. 363

IRA. In 1920 Sean attended the Treaty negotiations, as aide-de-camp to Michael Collins, but he opposed the Treaty itself, just as the ghosts required him to do, and was taken prisoner by Free State Government forces on the surrender of the Four Courts in the summer of 1922. When the civil war was over, in 1923, Sean became Chief of Staff of the IRA, now gone underground. By this move, he was singling himself out as a better Republican than de Valera and his colleagues, who never forgave this. Sean seems to have ended his active connection with the IRA about 1925, but he remained a sympathiser, and eminent member of the Republican movement all his life. Brought up as he was, he could hardly have done otherwise.

The launching of Clann na Poblachta, in the late forties, was done in concert with the IRA, though this was never explicitly acknowledged.

In the elections of 1948, MacBride's Clann na Poblachta won the balance of power in the new Dáil, and this resulted in a coalition, of which the main components were Fine Gael (the old Treaty party), Labour and the Clann itself, with Sean MacBride as Minister for External Affairs. Normally, the alliance with Fine Gael would have been most distasteful to Republican supporters, but this time it was accepted as a regrettable necessity in order to put Fianna Fáil out of power. MacBride now induced the new coalition to pass the Republic of Ireland Act 1949. This was a change of name only, since the territorial jurisdiction of the Republic remained the same as that of the old Free State, and the Constitution was still de Valera's 1937 one. But the move was politically astute. On behalf of both MacBride and the Taoiseach John A Costello, the enactment of the Republic made an anti-Dev point. De Valera called himself a Republican, but had never actually *declared* a Republic, though he could have done so. Dev's reason for refraining from this was that to take this step would close the door against eventual negotiations with Northern Ireland. This was not, however, an argument that could cut much ice with the Catholic and nationalist electorate. Dev did not press the point, and preserved a Sphinx-like profile. That door closed.

Hard-line Republicans (ie the IRA) could not possibly be satisfied by the Costello-MacBride Republic: the Irish Free State under a new name. But they were ready to accept it as a step in the right direction. It did not suit them to crab a coalition with Sean MacBride in it. De Valera's government had got very rough with Republicans. They had reason to feel sure that a government with Sean MacBride in it would never get that way.[71] So the more clout MacBride had in the coalition, the better. The Republic of Ireland Act demonstrated MacBride's clout, and so was not to be despised.

There was another factor working to endear that Republic to the IRA. Costello's argument in favour of it was that it would "take the gun out of politics". The IRA had their own ideas about how the gun might eventually be taken out of politics. But *as a tendency on the part of the Government*, a policy of "taking the gun out of politics" by manifestations of deference towards the feelings of the IRA had much to be said for it. It was vastly preferable to de Valera's war-time formula for taking the gun out of politics, through internment, executions and letting hunger-strikers die. So on the whole, the IRA was in favour of giving the Costello-MacBride coalition an easy ride. In any case the IRA itself, in the aftermath of the Second World War, was in some need of repose and reorganisation after its gruelling war-time experiences at the hands of the de Valera Government.

In the retrospect of nearly half a century later, we can see that the Costello Government's "taking the gun out of politics" by enacting the Republic, was an early manifestation of the sort of thinking that has given us "the peace process" of 1993-4. That is to say, you give the IRA a bit of what they want, in the hope that they will be so pleased with the bit that they will stop, without holding out for the whole. In other contexts such a policy has been known as appeasement. It does not

---

71. For MacBride's IRA connections at this time, see Dermot Keogh, *Twentieth-Century Ireland* (Dublin 1994) pp. 173-4

have an impressive international track-record.

I served under MacBride at the Department of External Affairs from 1948-51 and was in frequent contact with him, since he put me in charge of a newly-established Information Section in the Department. I found him a courteous and considerate person to work with. You could sense the presence of ghosts all right; his face, when in repose, had a perpetually haunted expression like his mother's. Indeed his features, in middle age, had an uncanny resemblance to his mother's *in old age*: the large and lustrous eyes, the hollow cheeks, the pallor, and the salience of the skull beneath the skin. He looked, in Yeats's words, like a being who "took a mess of shadows for its meat".

He didn't though; appearances were deceptive in that respect; he must have had a marvellous metabolism. He was a notable gourmet and connoisseur of wine. He also liked women, and pursued them even at an advanced age, in the course of the international career which was to bring, to the former Chief of Staff of the IRA, both the Nobel Peace Prize and the Lenin Peace Prize. At that stage, his combination of an amorous disposition with what was by then a spectacularly sepulchral appearance earned him a nickname among the female members of the international press corps (as I learned much later from one of them). The nickname was, "Death Takes a Holiday".

Looking back on it, I have an impression that Sean had managed to strike a kind of bargain with those ghosts. That, if he would always do what they required of him in Irish politics – by always helping the IRA – they would let him alone in every other respect. This was a bad bargain as far as Irish politics was concerned. But one can hardly blame Sean for striking it, when one thinks of the circumstances of his childhood and boyhood. In dealing with ghosts, practice makes perfect. Like her son, Maud Gonne lived to an advanced age in a perennially funereal manner.

The immediate consequence of the Republic of Ireland Act was the passage of the Ireland Act, a measure introduced by the Attlee Government, reaffirming Northern Ireland's status as part of the United Kingdom. This was an inevitable response (at that time) to the Republic of Ireland Act, and the nationalist response to the Ireland Act was equally inevitable: a storm of protest, supported by all nationalist parties, and followed by a prolonged outpouring of propaganda, all vociferously challenging the legitimacy of Northern Ireland's existence. De Valera was visibly unenthusiastic about all this, but felt constrained, by his own past commitments since 1925, by his own Constitution, and by the popular mood, to give the campaign his nominal support. Personally he supported it in Australia. The whole campaign served no purposes except those of the IRA, since the message it conveyed was that Northern Ireland was so illegitimate and so obnoxious that it must at all costs be removed. And if the British would not remove it, then it would be their own fault if others began to remove it by force. A line of thought that a substantial if fluctuating, minority – and perhaps even a majority, at some levels of the psyche – still finds persuasive.

I played a minor, but not insignificant part in all this. As Head of the Information Section of the Department of External Affairs, under Sean MacBride, it was my job to do so. I edited the Department's Weekly Bulletin, which of course featured MacBride's speeches prominently, and some of those speeches were written by me. Later, I came to look back on this phase of my career with growing distaste, but I can't say I felt any qualms about it at the time. I realised fairly early that the anti-partition campaign was doing no good, but it took me a lot longer to realise that it was doing serious harm. I didn't come to a full realisation of this until the Provisional IRA offensive began, a good many years afterwards, early in 1971.

As I look back on all that, in the context of preparing this study, I feel a certain rueful sympathy with my father's position, in relation to the Great Twist, in the early 1900's. We were both, inadvertently and marginally, part of the invisible empire of the ghosts of the nation. My father had shaken that

137

off, almost entirely, before he died in 1927. It took me longer, but I'm glad to have made it, finally.

In any case, in the great upsurge of propaganda that followed the Ireland Act, the main responsibility for anti-partition activities was taken away from the Department of External Affairs and given to a group headed by the late Frank Gallagher, de Valera's principal assistant in press and propaganda affairs. This group met in the Mansion House, under the general authority of an All-Party Committee. I attended the first meeting of that Committee, along with Sean MacBride. Thirteen years afterwards, when I was being seconded to UN service, and about to leave for Katanga, de Valera, then President, sent for me. The first thing he talked about was his memory of that meeting.

"It was at a time . . . when we were not in office . . . " Slight pause there, as if drawing a veil over a period of dubious legitimacy in Irish history. Dev went on: "Mr MacBride was Minister for External Affairs. You were there with him. Mr MacBride addressed the meeting. He spoke for some considerable time. I noticed that, while he was speaking, you were not watching him. You were watching me. And I said to myself: 'That young man is . . . interested in politics.'"

He realised that this surprised me, for he went on: "I know you thought I couldn't see you for I was supposed to be blind. So I was, very nearly, but at that time I still had what they called peripheral vision . . . That is to say, I could see out the corner of my eyes."

Dev then produced his famous smile, which had been likened (by an opponent) to "moonlight on a tombstone", but which was really rather shy and pleasant.

Soon after the Republic of Ireland Act rumpus, the Costello-MacBride coalition was in deep trouble. The reasons for this had nothing directly to do with the rumpus over the Ireland Act, but they did have a lot to do with religion and nationalism. The occasion for the trouble was a Mother-and-Child Health Scheme introduced by Dr Noel Browne, Minister for Health in the coalition and a member of Sean MacBride's Clann na Poblachta, which was itself a kind of coalition between old-style Republicans and younger radicals, attracted by what they regarded as Republican idealism. Being politically inexperienced, these young radicals tended to take literally a certain Republican rhetoric which sounds liberal at a distance, owing to an anti-clerical component which is entirely due to past clashes with the Church over political violence. Republicans, being intensely authoritarian themselves, have no objection to the authoritarianism of the Church except in the narrow, and deviously contested, area where it conflicts with their own variety, as it sometimes does, not always.

However the young radicals in the Party may have felt, Clann na Poblachta policy, as presented to the public, was Catholic-nationalist, very much in line with the Irish Ireland of the early part of the century. The Clann was bent on resisting "the alien, artificial and unchristian concepts of life,"[72] DP Moran's programme exactly. Sean MacBride as leader of Clann na Poblachta and Minister for External Affairs of the Republic was at some pains to emphasise his personal Catholicism. When there was work to be done on a Sunday – as often happened – he would show up at Iveagh House clutching his Missal. As Honor Tracy wrote, about this time: "Ireland is a country where Mr Sean MacBride goes to Mass."

The new inter-Party Government, with Clann na Poblachta in it, sent to the Vatican, from its first Cabinet meeting, the most effusively Catholic message ever sent by any Government of the Irish State, since its foundation in 1921. Their telegram desired "to repose at the feet of your Holiness the assurance of our filial loyalty and of our devotion to your August Person, as well as our firm resolve to be guided in all our work by the teaching of Christ, and to strive for the attainment of a social order in Ireland based on Christian principles".[73] This was a Catholic-nationalist Government with an unusually strong and explicit emphasis on the "Catholic". It

---

72. Keogh, *Twentieth-Century Ireland*, p. 175
73. Keogh, *Twentieth Century Ireland*, p. 187

was also the first Government, since the State was founded, to be strongly influenced by the IRA. The first, but not the last.

Dermot Keogh describes Dr Noel Browne as "a somewhat irregular attender at Cabinet meetings" and I assume that he was not present at the meeting where the "repose at the feet" message was approved. But the message gives a vivid impression of the spiritual-political background to the later handling, by John A Costello and Sean MacBride, of Dr Browne's Mother and Child Health Scheme.

Dr Browne was, and is, a person of passionate social concern, and he was determined to use his position in the Coalition to help the poor and disadvantaged. His contribution to the fight against tuberculosis was generally admired, and he followed this up with a Mother-and-Child Health Scheme, without a means test. This was an expensive measure, and unpopular with the medical profession. For both these reasons, it was also unpopular with the Fine Gael party, much the most important partner in the then Government, numerically speaking.

John A Costello, the head of the Coalition Government, in an effort to quash Browne's scheme, called in the help of the Catholic Church. He must have known, through the doctors, that churchmen had at least serious doubts about the scheme. In Ireland, senior Catholic members of the medical profession have very close relations with the Catholic clergy. This is a country in which theology and obstetrics overlap, and consequently one in which it is both eschatologically and professionally beneficial for doctors – especially but not exclusively, gynaecologists – to be known to be on good terms with the Church. This connection is often rewarding for both sides. On this occasion, it was rewarding to the doctors, but less so to the Church.

Costello announced that, in his concern over whether the measure proposed to his Government was morally sound, he had consulted the Catholic Archbishop of Dublin, John Charles McQuaid. Dr McQuaid had advised him that a Mother-and-Child health scheme without a means test was "contrary to the moral teaching of the Church". Costello made it known that for him, as a faithful son of the Church, it was unthinkable that he could be responsible for recommending such a measure to the Dáil. He had therefore asked the responsible Minister, Dr Browne, to amend his scheme in such a manner as to bring it into line with the moral teaching of the Church. Sean MacBride, the leader of Dr Browne's party, backed Costello, and the Clann na Poblachta parliamentary party backed MacBride. Dr Browne was on his own. He later recalled the harsh questioning to which he had been subjected by strong Republicans in the Party. The main thing was that the Costello-MacBride government was satisfactory to the Republican movement, in its narrow sense, of which the core is always the IRA. Dr Browne was caught in a pincers: religion and nationalism converging.

Dr Browne's leader, Sean MacBride, ordered Dr Browne to comply with the Taoiseach's directive. On Dr Browne's refusal to do so, MacBride demanded and obtained Dr Browne's resignation. The Government fell, and in the ensuing elections the main loser was MacBride's Clann na Poblachta Party. It was reduced from ten seats to two: MacBride himself and one other. The Party dissolved completely, not long afterwards. It was clear that MacBride, himself a Republican romantic, had grossly overestimated the electoral strength of the Republican component, as distinct from the vaguely progressive and faintly anti-clerical component, in the support for his party. The Republicans would have to find other channels and they eventually did.

The episode was atypical, in its blatancy. Issues were aired which were, and are, normally discussed behind closed doors. To outsiders, it looked like a case of the Church dictating to the State. It was actually a case of a politician asking for a *public* intervention by the Church, for political reasons, and spectacularly bungling the whole business. This is not the way the culture works and those who went against the grain of the culture paid the penalty. Both the Church and the Republican movement operate most successfully by indirection: saying one thing, while implying another, and meaning, perhaps, a third. By the late twentieth century religion and nationalism, the two great forces in the culture, had achieved a highly sophisticated form of intercommunication and interaction along those lines.

Here, I am using the expression "the Republican movement" in its broadest sense, as including the largest party in the Republic, Fianna Fáil, whose name in English is "the Republican Party". Fianna Fáil people – and many in the other constitutional parties also – hear the same ancestral voices as does the Republican movement in its narrowest sense consisting solely of Sinn Féin-IRA. The broad Republican movement hears those voices more faintly than does the narrow one: more faintly, less imperatively, and to more ambiguous effect. But the faint voices insidiously abet the louder and more imperious ones, so that Sinn Fein-IRA has always much more influence than the amount of overt support accorded to it at any given time would lead one to believe.

The overt support, for Sinn Féin in the Republic, is tiny; less than two per cent in national elections (1992) and negligible also in the polls: with over 90% calling for an end to political violence in an early 1994 poll. But the forces we are dealing with here are not readily quantifiable or readily controlled by quantification.

Even within the Republican movement in its narrower sense, there is a hierarchy of similar character. Those who are actually fighting for Ireland in the here and now, have an ascendancy over those who are not. Thus, in 1948, Sean MacBride, though a member of the democratically elected government, felt himself to be under the authority of the IRA Army Council: that was part of the bargain with the ghosts. I think Sean MacBride joined in the firing of Noel Browne, not because Costello told him to, nor out of genuine submission to Catholic teaching, but because the IRA told him to. The preservation of that coalition was in the interests of the IRA, for the discharge of their mandate from the dead, which greatly transcended any stuff about mothers and children. MacBride fully understood that: it is the value-system of *Cathleen ni Houlihan*: *Michael breaks away from Delia*, just as Sean's mother planned it.

As for Dr Browne, he remained, after the Mother-and-Child debâcle, a greatly respected but politically-isolated figure, opposed as he now found himself to be, both to the political influence of the Catholic Church, and to the Republican movement. As the old Fenian John O'Leary had told the young WB Yeats: "In this country a man must have either the Church or the Fenians on his side . . ."[74] Dr Browne, after his Mother-and-Child ordeal, had neither. For an Irish Catholic, a collision with the institutional Catholic Church in the mid-twentieth century was no light matter. But the other rejection perhaps hurt more. Dr Browne's repudiation at the hands of his own leader and his Republican colleagues had been peculiarly painful to him. Long afterwards, in 1969-70, he and I, being then members of the Parliamentary Labour Party, shared an office in Leinster House with two other Labour Party TD's. One day in the summer of 1970 I was sitting in that office, writing something about the ominous forces then taking shape in and around Northern Ireland, when Noel Browne came in. Noel and I already had our political differences (not relevant here) but I was aware that we had one important thing in common: both of us had felt constrained to ignore John O'Leary's politic and weighty advice. On an impulse, I put to Noel the question:

"Noel, if you were obliged to choose between Holy Mother Church and Cathleen ni Houlihan, which of the two would you prefer?"

Without an instant's hesitation, Noel Browne replied: "Holy Mother Church, every time!"

Me too.

---

74. O'Leary had added "and you will never have the Church", meaning that Yeats, whom he was addressing, was a Protestant. Noel Browne, being a Catholic, could have "had the Church" but only at the price of an obedience, in a political matter, which he could not accord.

Yet one doesn't often have a clear choice. Holy Mother and Cathleen are often in cahoots: as with Cardinal Cullen and the Christian Brothers as in the aftermath of 1916, as in clerical acquiescence in a cult of the Proclamation. And above all in a common denial of the legitimacy of Northern Ireland. Together, but always deniably so, the two have maintained the pressure on the Ulster Protestants over decades, and brought it to the point where we now seem to be approaching the verge of civil war.

LOOKING GHOSTS IN THE EYE: FRANK AIKEN, SEAN LEMASS AND SEAN MACENTEE

That is the point we seem to have reached, more or less, as I write this, in the late summer of 1994. Yet there was a period, and not so long ago, when Irish politics seemed to be moving in a quite different direction: a time in which political leaders in the Republic seriously sought accommodation with unionist leaders, and were prepared, and equipped, to resist the Catholic-nationalist territorial drive.

The period was approximately 1956-1966. This was the period that saw the retirement of Eamon de Valera from active politics. The political leaders in question were de Valera's principal lieutenants: Frank Aiken, Sean Lemass and Sean MacEntee. They differed in many ways, both temperamentally and politically, and there were rivalries between them. But they had certain vital things in common. They wanted a decent, and mutually respectful, relation between Catholics and Protestants, nationalists and unionists, in the island of Ireland. They were not prepared to render unconditional obeisance either to Holy Mother Church or to Cathleen ni Houlihan, although they were adept at handling both of these. And they were implacably resolved not to allow the IRA either to dictate to the democratic government or to usurp its powers.

The three had advantages denied to a later generation of political leaders (such as Jack Lynch, who shared, on the whole, their political outlook). Their own Republican credentials were impeccable. Lemass and MacEntee were veterans of 1916: Aiken had been the last Chief of Staff of the Republican (or "Irregular") side in the Irish Civil War of 1922-3. They had influence proportionate to their record. They were also, to the same extent, stuck with the nationalist rhetoric that was part of Fianna Fáil's political stock-in-trade especially when it was out of office. But they didn't, as it were, inhale. They could hear ancestral voices as well as anyone, but in their mature years they never allowed the voices to take control. They had seen, in the Civil War, what happened when the voices did, and they wanted no more of that. They wanted relations with Ulster Protestants to get better, not worse, and they realised that the strident anti-partition propaganda unleashed by the Ireland Act was making them worse. In the Council of Europe at Strasbourg, when some of the Irish delegates were sounding off on the usual lines, Sean MacEntee publicly rebuked them for bringing partition into everything "like a sore thumb".

Above all, the three were well aware that anti-partition propaganda, while intended for external consumption, had repercussions in Ireland itself, favourable to the post-Treaty IRA. Both they and de Valera were resolved that the elected Government, and not the IRA, with its mandate from the dead, should determine policy towards Northern Ireland. In 1957, the IRA started a new offensive against Northern Ireland. It offered the Government a bargain: it would respect the authority of the State, within the territory of the Republic, provided the State did not interfere there with the necessary preparations for operations against Northern Ireland (essentially the same as the secret Collins bargain of 1922). The Government's reply was uncompromising. By purporting to wage war on behalf of the Irish people, the IRA was usurping a basic function of Government. This would not be tolerated. The Government introduced internment and applied it efficiently, and the Gardai and the RUC cooperated closely against the IRA. This was exactly what the IRA had feared and tried to avert, in trying to save the Costello-MacBride Coalition in 1951. The IRA campaign fizzled out in 1962. I am convinced that if the later IRA offensive, beginning in 1971, had been met with the same determination in the Republic, it too could have been brought to an early end. But that was not to be.

The strength of these men was that each of them could look a Pearsean ghost in the eye, without batting an eye of their own. Each of them, in their youth, had done the thing the ghost asked them to do, in 1916 or in 1919-21 or both. That was it; from now on they would do what seemed reasonable to themselves in the interests of the actual people inhabiting the island of Ireland and not of a personified abstraction, or of a disembodied voice, or of a ghost. They did not need to dodge the ghosts, nor to seek to propitiate them. They were not impressed by the voices calling for blood. They had seen enough blood, and shed enough, themselves. If other persons believed they had a mandate from the dead, to take life, with no mandate from the living, these men had a mandate from the living to put such persons under restraint. That generation of Republican leaders could handle the ghosts, because they had settled their personal score with them by having done the thing the ghost had asked of them: once and for all. But what would happen when their generation passed from the scene? Might not the ghosts get out of hand, and "the blood-dimmed tide" of Yeats's "The Second Coming" be loosed again? We now know the answers to these questions. I shall come to them shortly.

I scarcely knew Sean Lemass, and I did not get to know Sean MacEntee well until the sixties (after I married his daughter, Maire). But I worked closely with Frank Aiken, in the Department of External Affairs, from the early fifties on and later became his closest adviser (mainly on UN matters). When the Costello-MacBride coalition fell as a result of the Browne affair, Fianna Fáil came back into office, with Aiken as Minister for External Affairs. Aiken took very seriously the Wolfe Tone doctrine of "the common name of Irishman" embracing "Catholics, Protestants and Dissenters", and he did not subscribe to the usual Republican reservation: "provided the Protestants and Dissenters stop being Unionists".

He was a Catholic and a nationalist but thought of these as two aspects of his belief-system, not as one conjoint thing. He was not, that is to say, a Catholic-nationalist, either of the school of DP Moran – whose national-sectarianism he would have detested – or of the far more exalted Catholic nationalism of Patrick Pearse. One sensed reservations about Pearse. Aiken quite often talked about Tone; never about Pearse.

Aiken was concerned about the then policy of abstention being pursued by the Northern nationalists, and he sent me North to convey his views to the nationalist leaders. In general, he thought that nationalists should not only stop abstaining from attending institutions to which they were elected, but should also take every opportunity of mingling with their Protestant neighbours.

Over several months, I paid a number of visits to the North and had several talks with the nationalist leaders of the time, notably Eddie McAteer in Derry and Gerry Lennon in Armagh. They received me kindly, and heard my message patiently. I remember Eddie McAteer smiling and saying, "Frank seems to have got a little out of touch". With Ulster, he meant. Aiken himself was a Catholic Ulsterman, as of course was Eddie McAteer.

On one of my last journeys on this congenial but rather forlorn mission, I called on a local nationalist leader in the Sperrin mountains. He was an old man, sitting on a box outside his little grocery store, staring out at the glen on that fine summer evening. Not very hopefully, I gave him the Aiken message. He said nothing, just stared glenward. For the sake of breaking the silence, I asked: "How many Protestants are there around here?" He replied, slowly and deliberately: "In this townland [rural district], we have only one Protestant . . . And with the help of God . . . we'll have him out of it by Christmas."

That old man was speaking for what Somerville and Ross cheerfully called "the spirit of the Nation". By which they meant religious bigotry: conjoined to nationalism on the Catholic side and to unionism on the Protestant.

A SHORT THAW AND THE END OF NELSON PILLAR

In the mid-sixties, there was a brief but remarkable thaw in relations between unionists and nationalists, Protestants and Catholics, in the island of Ireland. As Prime Minister of Northern Ireland, Terence O'Neill tried to fight the powerful sectarian element in Ulster unionism, and to end discrimination against Catholics. O'Neill was upper-class, educated in England, and with no trace of an Ulster accent. To many unionists, O'Neill seemed "out of touch", as Aiken did to Northern nationalists. Still, O'Neill was unionist leader, and his prestige was high, up to 1966.

Sean Lemass, who had succeeded de Valera as leader of Fianna Fáil, decided to meet O'Neill half way, and try to "normalise" relations between nationalists and unionists in the island of Ireland. In 1965, Lemass went to Belfast to meet O'Neill. This was the first meeting of the leaders of the two communities on the island, since the foundation of the two political entities within it in 1920-1921. The two leaders got on very well indeed. Basically, the understanding between them was that Northern Ireland would begin to end discrimination against Catholics, and that the Republic would cease to challenge the legitimacy of Northern Ireland. In the Republic, Lemass set in motion a process of constitutional review, which he intended to culminate in the amendment of Articles 2 and 3, in such a way as to end the territorial claim to Northern Ireland. Lemass's prestige among moderate unionists was high, because of his resolute stand against the IRA in 1957-62. So on the whole, the prospects for creative rapprochement between unionists and nationalists looked reasonably bright – considering the dark past – in 1965.

So what went wrong? The first thing that went wrong –

and the main thing in my opinion – was that the year following the Lemass-O'Neill meeting happened to be the fiftieth anniversary of the Rising of 1916. 1966 was a great commemorative year. Ghosts walked, and those ghosts cried out against peace with unionists. The effects were felt in somewhat different ways in the Republic and in Northern Ireland, but both sets of effects were profoundly subversive of the Lemass-O'Neill enterprise.

The general trend of the commemorative celebrations was unfavourable to the Lemass-O'Neill partnership, and favourable to the IRA. The IRA signified and symbolised their continuing presence and relevance in that year, and their contempt for any commemerative voices other than their own, by blowing up the most conspicuous monument on Dublin's main street, the Nelson Pillar.

In the Republic and over RTE especially, all who could be heard from were effusively rededicating themselves to the ideals of 1916. Those ideals, as expressed by Patrick Pearse, and literally understood, were incompatible with the recognition of the legitimacy of Northern Ireland, with the rescinding of the territorial claim contained in Articles 2 and 3, or with any kind of compromise. Patrick Pearse had said (in *Ghosts*):

"Irish nationality . . . has meant not the freedom of a geographical fragment of Ireland, but the freedom of Ireland, of every sod of Ireland." That meant that "Ireland" was not free as long as Northern Ireland existed and was part of the United Kingdom. And Patrick Pearse had also said, by the grave of O'Donovan Rossa, in August, 1915: "and while Ireland holds these graves, Ireland unfree shall never be at peace". Taken together, those two statements constitute a mandate, from those who died for Ireland, for war against the British and the majority in Northern Ireland. Sean Lemass had no intention of allowing his government to be dominated by *obiter dicta* from Patrick Pearse and the ghosts he had "raised" on Christmas Day, 1915 (see epigraph). All the same, those ghosts, long joined by the ghost of Pearse himself, were being empowered, in 1966, by the rites of commemoration of the sacralised dead.

The damage done to Lemass-O'Neill by the commemorative ceremonies in the Republic was great, but might not necessarily have been fatal. It was the combined effect of those celebrations and their repercussions inside Northern Ireland that was to nip the hopes of 1965 in the bud.

About ten years later, I met Terence O'Neill, at a luncheon in Guinness's Brewery, Dublin. He had been forced out of office long before and was now Lord O'Neill of the Maine. I asked him what part the commemorations of 1916 had played in the destruction of his hopes. He told me the role of the commemorations had been decisive. Not the ceremonies and so on in the Republic, which were not helpful, but would not have been deeply damaging, if they could have been kept offstage. It was the repercussions inside Northern Ireland that fatally weakened O'Neill. "All of a sudden there were all those flags, you see. All over the Catholic areas. Tricolours. This was against the law."

Under the Flags and Emblems Act (Northern Ireland) the flying of the tricolour was illegal in Northern Ireland. The tricolour – green, white and orange – is supposed to symbolise peace between the two traditions but cannot be flown, where the two traditions are both actually present, without precipitating a riot. Also, in Northern Ireland, those who regard it as their flag (Catholics), never refer to "orange" as one of its colours. It is "green, white and gold", "green, white and yellow" or "green, white and saffron". Never "orange". The oecumenical (or pseudo-oecumenical) symbolism of the flag goes against the emotional grain of the Catholic-nationalist reality. This is a sort of litmus test of Irish nationalism.

O'Neill went on: "All those displays were illegal. But I ordered the RUC not to interfere with them. I knew that if they did, that would undo what Sean Lemass was trying to do. But by failing to enforce the law, where it was openly defied, I was destroying my influence among my own people".

It wasn't only the breach of the law, though that was

important. There was also the intrinsic symbolism of the flags, which would have been there even if it had been legal to fly them. Those flags, flying all over the Catholic areas, symbolised (in reality as distinct from theory) the identity of religion and nationalism among the Catholics of Northern Ireland. Not among all Catholics, but enough to make that identity a formidable fact.

Traditionally, unionists had justified discrimination against Catholics, on the ground that these were all really nationalists, hostile to the existence of Northern Ireland. O'Neill had argued against all that. But all those flags seemed to be saying that the traditional unionists were right on that point. The credibility of the hardliners rose proportionately and O'Neill's fell. A long frost was to follow the O'Neill brief thaw.

THE NATIONAL TERRITORY

In these final sections of *Ancestral Voices* I shall briefly consider, in relation to the two forces with which we are concerned, the history and interaction of the two new politic entities which came into being in the island of Ireland in 1920-21. Northern Ireland was created in 1920, by the Government of Ireland Act of that year. It consisted, and consists today, of the six north-eastern counties of the island. The other entity, created by the Anglo-Irish Treaty of December, 1921, was known originally as the Irish Free State. Since 1949, it has been known as the Republic of Ireland, whose territory and most other characteristics are identical with those of the Free State.

The population of the Republic is today overwhelmingly Catholic. The Protestant minority was around 12% when the Irish Free State came into being. The proportion shrank over the years, as a result first of emigration of British officials and others, and then of intermarriage. Almost all ecclesiastically "mixed" marriages are governed by Catholic regulations, so that almost all the children of such marriages are brought up as Catholics. Under these conditions (as well as through emigration) the proportion of Protestants in the Republic shrank from around 12% in 1921 to around 3% today.

When Northern Ireland was set up, Catholics were about one-third of the population. They are now believed to be around 40%. (It is hard to be quite certain, as census-taking in Northern Ireland has become a hazardous occupation.)

Nationalists are in the habit of referring to the "artificial partition" of the island. In principle, there is nothing artificial about the partition: it is a result of history, traditions and demography. When Catholics decided to secede from the United Kingdom, Protestants seceded from the secession. (Similar things are happening today, in many parts of the former Soviet Union.) There is nothing artificial about partition. But there *is* something artificial about the actual boundary. If the boundary had been drawn by an impartial commission, quite large tracts of land on the Border, with sizeable populations, would have been awarded to the Free State. Northern Ireland today would be a smaller entity, and possibly a more stable one. But once the nationalists refused even to discuss partition, the unionists got the boundary they wanted, and thought they needed.

Partition is not artificial nor is it unjust, in itself. But the actual partition settlement of 1920-21 had the seeds of injustice in it (not mainly because of the boundary) and the seeds duly germinated. Originally, the Ulster unionists had asked simply to be allowed to remain in the United Kingdom: they had not asked for a separate Parliament. But the British Government decided that both parts of Ireland must have Parliaments. This decision stemmed from a desire on the part of British politicians to rid themselves of as much responsibility for Ireland as they could. The British couldn't just kick the unionists out of the United Kingdom; not yet, anyway. But they could, as it were, keep them on a kind of reservation within it, known as Stormont.

The great attraction of the whole deal, from the point of view of the British Government and Parliament was that, since the two lots of troublesome Irish now had Parliaments of their own, questions about Ireland would no longer, in most circumstances, have to be answered in the Imperial Parliament. What a relief!

I think that when Lloyd George's Government worked out the deal with the two Parliaments in it, they probably expected that the minorities, in both jurisdictions, would have a pretty rough time. Lloyd George didn't have to worry about that, since he could normally expect to be able to avoid answering questions about it in Parliament. In the event, only one of the minorities got what could reasonably be regarded as a rough time. The Protestant minority in what is now the Republic fared quite well. The Catholic minority in Northern Ireland did not.

This differential did not arise from a contrast in national and religious character – Catholics/nationalists being nice, while Protestants/unionists are nasty – although that has always been the explanation favoured by Catholics and nationalists. As far as my own observations allow me to judge, Original Sin is evenly distributed between the two communities. The differential arises from the respective sizes and dispositions of the two minority communities. The Protestant minority in the Republic is small and has never sought to subvert the institutions of the State. The Catholic minority in Northern Ireland is large and many of its members – perhaps most – regard Northern Ireland as an illegitimate entity. A minority, within the minority, claim the right to destroy Northern Ireland by force. And the minority-within-the-minority is harboured and protected by the minority as a whole.

There are two political parties in Northern Ireland based on the Catholic community: the Social Democratic and Labour Party and Sinn Féin. The SDLP refrains from recommending its supporters to co-operate with the security forces, on a regular basis, although it has on occasion recommended its supporters to co-operate in the apprehension of the perpetrators of a particular atrocity. Sinn Féin expects its supporters to co-operate with the IRA, which they do.

Had the Protestant minority in the Republic been of equivalent size, and possessed equivalent characteristics, it would certainly have been dealt with by Governments of the Republic at least as harshly as the Catholics of Northern Ireland were dealt with by Stormont. As it was, that didn't happen; there was simply no need for it.

In Northern Ireland, the Stormont Government, for the duration of its existence – 1920 to 1972 – used such powers as it had for the advantage of Protestants and the disadvantage of Catholics. The powers devolved to Stormont were limited, and the official discrimination suffered by Catholics occurred mainly in the areas of public service jobs, housing and local government franchise. The oppression of Catholics was not as fearsome as nationalist propaganda suggested, but there is no doubt that Catholics were treated as second-class citizens and knew their condition to be unique in the United Kingdom. Their resentment was proportionate to this.

Their resentment was fuelled – and in some cases fanned to fury – by certain symbolic patterns, also peculiar to the area. Specifically, if there had been no Stormont, the Union Jack could have been seen simply as the flag of the United Kingdom. Catholics could have gone on living with that, as they had done for generations. But under Stormont, the Union Jack and the British national anthem were systematically used as symbols of Protestant dominion over Catholics. In this symbolism, the interactions of religion and nationalism assumed ominously pathological forms. Dragon's teeth were sown, that were to spring up armed men.

In the early years of the Irish Free State, religion and nationalism appeared to be in conflict: the uncompromising nationalists were under the ban of the Church. Yet the divergence was always more apparent than real, and it faded altogether after Eamon de Valera rose to power in 1932. De Valera's 1937 Constitution represented an adroit conjuncture of religion and nationalism. It recognised the Roman Catholic church as the "guardian of the faith professed by the great majority of the citizens".[75] It also laid claim, *de jure*, to the territory of Northern Ireland. Article 2 declared the national territory to consist of "'the whole island of Ireland, its islands and the territorial seas". Article 3 suspended the *de facto* implementation of the territorial claim, "pending the reintegration of the national territory". The Constitution embodying these propositions was put to the electorate of the then Free State (Twenty-six Counties) and enacted by them. The Articles are still in force and the reintegration of the national territory was ruled by the Irish Supreme Court (in January 1990) to be a "constitutional imperative". It is not clear on what grounds the Supreme Court reached this decision, unexpected by and unwelcome to moderate nationalists. Possibly the Court had heard *in camera* the deposition of a Pearsean ghost, and bowed to the Pearsean imperative: "you must do the thing it asks you". It seems improbable that de Valera saw it in that light in 1937. If he did, after all, he could have made his Constitution say so, which it didn't.

The effect, and probably also the purpose, of de Valera's Constitution was to put his party, Fianna Fáil, firmly at the centre of the Irish spectrum, in respect both of religion and of nationalism. The Constitution was more Catholic than its predecessor. The original Free State Constitution was secular in form; being based on the Anglo-Irish Treaty, it had to be. So, for de Valera to show himself, through his Constitution, to be a better Catholic than the politicians who had depicted him as a bad one, was a brilliant stroke.

So much for religion, in de Valera's Constitution. In respect of nationalism, too, the Constitution was exceedingly well tailored to the tastes of the Twenty-Six County electorate. Article 2 was pure nationalist doctrine. But Article 3 signalled that Fianna Fáil was not about to start a new civil war. An

---

75. The Article in question was later withdrawn by Referendum having been found by the Church itself to be surplus to requirements. But the Constitution remained Catholic in spirit. In its present form (1994), it still prohibits legislation permitting divorce, and contains a proviso, of recent origin, intended to prohibit legislation permitting abortion.

electorate that could still remember the horrors of 1919-23 needed to be reassured on that point. It should be noted also that, while de Valera's Constitution is both Catholic and nationalist, it keeps the two aspects in separate compartments; there is no direct suggestion of the Pearsean fusion or even of the explicit Catholic nationalism of Irish Ireland. It remains true that the Constitution was enacted by the overwhelmingly Catholic population of the Twenty-six Counties (or rather on behalf of these, since a great many of them did not bother to vote.) It was deemed to be binding *de jure* on everyone in the island, although it was known that a majority of the population of Northern Ireland was bitterly opposed to it. Their objections and indeed their existence were silently treated as irrelevant. This was not a transaction that boded well for future relations between what nationalists later came to call "the two traditions" in Ireland.

In office, de Valera did nothing to secure the reintegration of the national territory. His main assertion of nationalism, in practice as distinct from precept, was his policy of neutrality in the Second World War. His immediate successors in the leadership of Fianna Fáil tried to hold irredentist nationalism in check and to reach accommodation with the unionist leadership.

FROM CIVIL RIGHTS TO THE PROVISIONALS

The period from 1966 to 1969 was the heyday of the civil rights movement in Northern Ireland. In appearance and in rhetoric, this movement had nothing whatever to do with either Catholicism or nationalism. In reality, it was heavily impregnated with both.

The generation of Catholics that grew up in Northern Ireland under the Welfare State was better fed, better off and better educated than any previous generation had been. Before the War, it had been rare for any Catholic to get a university education. Now many Catholics were entering universities and graduating from them. These were determined not to accept second-class status as their parents had done. They were well-informed about the world outside and capable of learning from it. The main relevant example before them was that of the American civil rights movement, as it operated in Dixie. The civil rights workers had staged protests in the Southern States against the racist institutions and laws. The violent repressions of these protests by State police were picked up by television and carried into the Northern States, where they produced a wave of revulsion that was to destroy the racist institutions and laws in the South.

The civil rights movement in Northern Ireland decided to apply the same techniques, but this time in order to reach the television audience in mainland Britain. It seemed a sound policy, and it worked to perfection, up to a point, after which the Irish model deviated sharply from the American model, as a result of a totally unforeseen interaction of religious and nationalist forces.

As already indicated, the civil rights movement, while made up almost entirely of nationalist Catholics, did not use Catholic or nationalist rhetoric. That would have been inappropriate, since the people they wanted to reach were British Protestants and post-Protestants. In any case, these young people – at that time – felt themselves to be thoroughly modern, and emancipated both from traditional Catholicism and traditional nationalism. This air of total modernity and emancipation among people who, at one level of their psyche, are heeding the imperatives of the Pearsean ghosts has long outlasted the civil rights movement. It is a chronic and chronically misleading feature of modern Irish Catholic nationalism. That the Catholic bit should be soft-pedalled, in a political context, was nothing new. "Anti-sectarian" or "non-sectarian" had long been a code-word for "Catholic", having the advantage of pinning the repellent "sectarian" label securely and exclusively on the Protestants. What was new, however – and a great novelty it was among Catholics in Northern Ireland – was a bold disavowal of *nationalism*. The civil rights demand was for "full British rights".

In consequence of the civil rights movement and its increasingly violent repression by Stormont, British troops were deployed in Belfast and Derry, in August 1969, "in support of the civil power". This meant that the Government of the United Kingdom was taking control of security in Northern Ireland, and that the end of the road was in sight for Stormont. This looked like a great victory for civil rights. But in the moment of victory, civil rights turned into something else, as a result of a fateful new convergence of religion and nationalism.

A key component in the civil rights movement had been the IRA, then under "Marxist" leadership. Actually the then leader of the IRA, Cathal Goulding, had been more of a faithful follower of Wolfe Tone than of either Karl Marx or Patrick Pearse. He wanted to avoid sectarian strife. For this reason he discouraged displays of Catholicism in the ranks of the IRA. He sent a circular to his battalion commanders, instructing them that the saying of a decade of the rosary, long traditional at Republican funerals, was to be discontinued. Nine of these commanders returned the circular, indicating that it was not acceptable.

The Church disapproved of Goulding's Marxist leadership, seeing it as a recrudescence of that "irreligious nationalism" against which Paul Cullen and the Christian Brothers, among others, had struggled so effectively, and against which the Church remained vigilant. Local churchmen and constitutional nationalist politicians co-operated with members of the then Government in Dublin to encourage and finance a breakaway movement in the IRA, replacing irreligious nationalism with the religious kind: good Catholic nationalism. The Provisional IRA was founded. Among its leaders were the nine IRA commanders who had returned that circular about the Rosary.

The Provisionals have no qualms about sectarian civil war. They have been fighting a political-sectarian civil war now for nearly a quarter of a century. They have no Marxist or other secular hang-ups (although they occasionally pay lip-service to something they call "socialism"). They are Irish Catholics, fighting the Protestants and the British. Formally, they separate their Catholicism from their nationalism, rather as de Valera's constitution did. They have nothing against Protestants "as such", but *unionists* are legitimate targets. In Northern Ireland, the distinction between Protestants and unionists is no easier to sustain, in practice, than that between Catholics and nationalists.

The real (as distinct from the formal) ideology of the Provisionals is based on that so long inculcated by the Irish Christian Brothers and practised by Irish Ireland, but theirs is a fanatical modification of that ideology. It is true that the Provisionals seldom have recourse to Pearsean mystical-nationalist rhetoric. Most of them indeed, are probably not familiar with the main body of Pearse's writings. They do, however, know the speech at the grave of O'Donovan Rossa, and the fateful words: "And while Ireland holds these graves, Ireland unfree shall never be at peace". Formally, the ideology of the Provisionals is that of classical Irish Republicanism: a nominally secular ideology, descending from Wolfe Tone and the United Irish movement of the eighteenth century. Great as was the reverence accorded to Pearse after 1916, his mystical-nationalist writings never became canonical in the Republican tradition (and they have been repugnant even to some of Pearse's comrades). Yet all this is at the level of formal ideology, which is often less important than what people feel, and refrain from saying in public. It would be inaccurate to describe the Provisionals as possessing a Pearsean ideology. The reality is that the atavistic national-religious forces which moved Pearse, and moved through him, and became articulate in him, move the Provisionals also. Watch the Republican funerals, and especially those of the hunger-strikers. In short, the Provisionals hear the ghosts that call for blood, and they obey the call. They hear these voices, loud and strong, and are their instruments. Other nationalists – in the SDLP and in Fianna Fáil, chiefly – also hear these voices. But they hear them more faintly and refrain from obeying them, and they feel a little guilty about this. These other milder nationalists shrink from, and verbally condemn, the bloody deeds perpetrated by the servants of the ghosts. But inwardly, these milder nationalists feel the need to appease the ghosts, and to propitiate their servants. So the ghosts, directly and indirectly, are shaping the agenda of Irish nationalist politics in the late twentieth century. The vocabulary in which that agenda is usually expressed is impeccably modern, but the substance is obstinately archaic. We shall be seeing later, when we come to consider "the peace process", how peace itself, in Ireland, has been made the medium of the ghosts that call for blood.

In the Republic, 1969-70 saw a temporary but ominous revival of the Collins strategy for Northern Ireland: Governmental collusion with Catholic and nationalist guerrilla warfare there. The Lemass policy of 1957-62 was reversed by members of Jack Lynch's government. The IRA, in fighting against Northern Ireland, were no longer seen as usurping the functions of Government. They came to be seen, at least for a time, as covertly enforcing Government policy.

ANCESTRAL VOICES: LOUD AND FAINT

These developments were the result of the impact of perceived events in Northern Ireland on a new generation of politicians who had taken charge in the Republic, and specifically in Fianna Fáil. The founding generation of Fianna Fáil had passed from the scene of political activity by the late sixties. De Valera had become President, a largely ceremonial office, without executive power. Sean Lemass and Frank Aiken had retired from public life. This meant that the generation of leadership which could look those ghosts in the eye and coolly say "no" had now departed from the scene. This was a more momentous transition than appeared at the time.

The other generation had, as it were, been vaccinated against the ancestral voices. The younger generation had no such immunity. They could hear the voices, in varying strengths, but had no idea about how to handle them. They had inherited a rhetoric which validated the voices. They didn't know much Irish history but they assumed that what they did know was all that was worth knowing. They hadn't read much Pearse, but they did know and felt that they approved what he had said at the grave of O'Donovan Rossa. They also knew the opening words (which are the most characteristically Pearsean) of the Proclamation of the Republic. "In the name of God and of the dead generations from which she receives her old tradition of nationhood . . . "

So these men, new to power, were conditioned to hear the ancestral voices with respect; and without any of the suspicion which their immediate precedessors had learned from experience. The new people had no relevant experience, just a confident assumption that they knew everything that was relevant.

As we have seen, it is not just a question of hearing voices. It is also a question of how loudly different kinds of nationalists hear the voices, and how the differential in the volume of reception affects relationships between the nationalists in question. Unless there is acquired immunity (as in the case of the senior Fianna Fáil politicians already considered), the nationalist who is hearing the voices loudly will have a psychological, moral and political ascendancy over the nationalist who is hearing them only faintly. The Dublin Government's involvement with Northern Ireland in 1969-70 clearly illustrated this phenomenon.

The most significant members of that Government during that period were: Jack Lynch (Taoiseach), Charles J Haughey (Minister for Finance) Neil Blaney and Kevin Boland (the portfolios of the last two were not relevant to their contributions to decision-making over Northern Ireland).

Now, if there were the equivalent of a Richter Scale in relation to the volume of reception of ancestral voices, these politicians would rate on that scale roughly as follows:

Jack Lynch	2
CJ Haughey	3-4 (?)
Neil Blaney and Kevin Boland	7-8

Jack Lynch was a compromise choice as Taoiseach. He was a great sportsman and very popular in the country, especially in his native Cork. But his Fianna Fáil credentials were not strong and he was suspect in the eyes of the Party's Republican wing (as would appear from his rating on that scale).

Events in August 1969 in Northern Ireland activated the voices to a degree in which the relative ratings of those politicians on that scale came to be of decisive importance.

These were the Northern events that were to precipitate the deployment of the British troops and that led to the discrediting of the Official IRA and the emergence of the Provisionals. The train of violent events began when civil rights demonstrators stoned a (Protestant) traditional procession in Derry. Police then pursued the stone-throwers into the (Catholic) Bogside area of the city, where the police were met with defended barricades, and with petrol bombs. Catholics in Belfast began to riot to take the pressure off Derry. Protestant attacks on Catholics in Belfast followed on a larger scale accompanied by shooting. Units of the Northern Ireland police appeared to be helping the Protestant rioters (which was what led, almost immediately, to the deployment of British troops, to protect the Catholics).

Different audiences in Ireland watched these spectacular events on television, with the usual conflicting feelings and the usual mutual incomprehension. What Ulster Protestants saw was a Catholic revolt being resisted by the loyal Protestant population. What Catholics saw was an unprovoked assault by Protestants on Catholics, possibly with genocidal intent.

The Government in Dublin, being all Catholics and all responsible to a Catholic electorate, saw these transactions in the way that Catholics generally saw them. It was an occasion for ancestral voices to be heard, and for ghosts to walk and ask questions. But the most instructive feature of this situation was the working of the differential. This conferred authority, at this moment of crisis, on the fiercest nationalists, those who were deemed to be in the confidence of the ghostly voices. Blaney and Boland now demanded direct military intervention: Irish troops to enter Derry (which is part of Ireland's "national territory" under Article 2 of the Republic's Constitution). This demand, from that quarter, can hardly have surprised anyone, in the circumstances. What did surprise colleagues was that CJ Haughey supported the demand for military intervention. Haughey had not hitherto been regarded as a strong Republican (his father had been a Free State army officer during the Civil War of 1922-3), but rather as a cool pragmatist, like (in that respect) his father-in-law, Sean Lemass. But now, by joining the Blaney-Boland demand for military intervention, Haughey suddenly attains a rating of 7-8 degrees on the Richter Scale of ancestral-voice-reception. Some think this was a result of spontaneous indignation and outrage on his part, others that it was a matter of competing with Blaney in Republicanism, in case a Republican wave might make Blaney the successor to the leadership of Fianna Fáil. Either way, Haughey's shift testifies to the power of the voices, and the authority of those who seem to represent them.

Blaney and Haughey together were a formidable combination and Lynch felt obliged to give ground. He stopped short of invading Northern Ireland, but he took steps which amounted to the sanctioning of covert intervention there. He set up a committee of four on the affairs of Northern Ireland. Blaney and Haughey were two of the members; the other two were minor figures in the Fianna Fáil pecking order. Northern Ireland policy was under the control, from the autumn of 1969 to the early summer of 1970, of the two most extreme (or, in Mr Haughey's case, most seemingly-extreme) members of the Lynch Government. These now set about doing some of "the very big things" that the ghosts of a nation sometimes ask.

We do not know what all the very big things were, but the

principal fruit of them was the Provisional IRA, founded in this period, and armed and financed by Dublin, partly with money voted by the Dáil for the Relief of Distress in Northern Ireland and with the approval of Catholic Church authorities in Northern Ireland.

The period of actual governmental collaboration with the IRA ended in May 1970 after the Secretary of the Department of Justice, Peter Berry, informed the leader of the Opposition, Liam Cosgrave, of what was going on. Under pressure from the elder statesmen of his Party – de Valera, Aiken and MacEntee – Jack Lynch dismissed the two Ministers most directly involved, Neil Blaney and Charles J Haughey. The two politicians were later put on trial, not for anything they had done in Northern Ireland, but for importing arms illegally into the Republic. No case was found against Blaney, and Haughey was acquitted. At least one of Haughey's admirers, Fianna Fáil Deputy Niall Andrews, later saw him as Jesus Christ, wearing a Crown of Thorns and betrayed by Judas.

Despite the dismissals of the two Ministers, the policy they had been responsible for left permanent traces. When the Provisional IRA offensive against Northern Ireland began in February 1971, the Lynch Government, though now minus Haughey and Blaney, did not respond, as Lemass had done in 1957, with internment. To that extent, a bargain entered into in 1969, through Haughey and Blaney, was still unavowedly in force. As the IRA was active only in Northern Ireland and Britain, but not in the Republic, its members would not be interned in the Republic. They could be charged with offences, convicted and sentenced, but they would not be interned, provided the IRA remained quiet *in the Republic*. It was clearly understood (at that time) that, if they were not quiet in the Republic, internment would follow immediately. The Lemass-de Valera principle had been that an attempt to levy war in Northern Ireland was a usurpation of powers properly belonging to the Government of the Republic, and was therefore so grave a challenge that it must be met by internment. That principle was tacitly abandoned in those years and has never subsequently been reasserted, despite the initiation, in 1971, of IRA activity on a scale vastly exceeding anything before known.

In 1972, the Public Accounts Committee of the Dáil – an All Party body – found that moneys voted for the relief of distress in Northern Ireland had been applied to other purposes, including the purchase of arms. In 1973, as a member of the Cosgrave-Corish Coalition Government formed in that year, I proposed in Cabinet that a public enquiry be held into these various transactions. There was no support for this idea, and no overt opposition to it either. It just died, of silence. I was to experience the same type of silence a little later, over another matter. It was a silence that indicated that you were outside the Catholic consensus. In Northern Ireland, Protestants would welcome an enquiry of the kind proposed, and Catholics would not. So it suited the consensus that mystery should continue to shroud the origins of the Provisional IRA. After all, mystery and religion have been associated all through history. The least said, the better, especially in the great murky area where religion and nationalism overlap.

After Stormont was abolished, in 1972, Northern Ireland was ruled directly from Britain, as is still the case. But the British themselves didn't want this. Successive British Governments wanted to avoid responsibility for Northern Ireland, just as Lloyd George had done. Lloyd George's expedient for avoiding responsibility through Stormont, had failed. But the British looked – and are still looking – for something that could provide them with opportunities for such avoidance. The IRA are well aware of this, they work on it, and it helps to keep them going.

The first expedient tried by the British was cross-community devolution: the unionists and the SDLP – the "constitutional nationalists" – were to be partners in a devolved Executive. This seemed sensible, and for a time it looked like working. But the nationalist side – the SDLP and the Dublin Government under SDLP influence – insisted that devolved cross-community government from Northern Ireland was not enough. There must be recognition of what was called "the Irish dimension", meaning that there must be some symbolic harbinger of a United Ireland to come. So devolved cross-community government in Northern Ireland *plus* a Council of Ireland became the main ingredients of the agreement that was reached at Sunningdale, in 1974, between the Dublin and London Governments, the Unionists (then led by Brian Faulkner) and the SDLP.

I was a member of the Dublin Government at the time, and a member of that Government's negotiating team at Sunningdale. In Cabinet, I warned against the emphasis on the Council of Ireland. We were in danger of undermining our interlocutor. The important thing (I suggested) was to secure the cross-community Executive and ensure its survival. By piling on a lot of superfluous symbolism, we were in danger of capsizing the essential: the power-sharing Executive.

The then Minister for Foreign Affairs, Garret FitzGerald – briefed by John Hume – told the Cabinet that the danger I was warning against did not exist. The unionist community would accept Sunningdale, Council of Ireland and all. The Cabinet silently concurred. No problem. Next business.

I had a curious feeling at that meeting. It was not just a question of being in a minority of one on a point of policy. It was more a feeling of being in a minority of one, existentially: like being a member of a different species. I wanted to help the Faulkner Unionists, our partners in Sunningdale. That meant I didn't have the right gut-feelings about unionists-in-general. My colleagues had all had a good Catholic and nationalist education. I had been at a Protestant school, followed by Trinity College, at a time when Catholics were still prohibited from attending that institution. So I didn't know things that properly-educated people feel in their bones, without ever saying them in public. As, that the object of negotiating with unionists is not to get them off a hook, but to impale them on one. Not my fault that I didn't know all this, of course. Just one of those things. Perhaps my hearing was impaired. I couldn't (by this time) hear the voices that everybody else was hearing, however faintly.

The Executive survived for a few months, then collapsed under the pressure of the [Protestant] Ulster Workers' Council strike. Nationalists loudly complained about the British failure to suppress the strike by the use of military force. I could then see that it was not that nationalists (led and inspired by John Hume) had really failed to foresee the backlash, but that they had expected the British to deal with it forcefully. In that event, the unionists would be split, and their hardliners crushed. This doubly-desirable outcome would open the way for the final triumph of Catholics over Protestants in Ireland.

It was not to be; not that time round, but one can always keep trying.

By the late 1970's the IRA understood that there was no real will to defeat them, on the part of either Dublin or London. Dublin would not seriously incommode them, provided they kept quiet in the Republic. London was only looking, uneasily and indecisively, for ways of shedding direct responsibility for Northern Ireland, until the blessed day when it could disengage totally.

PATRICK PEARSE, BOBBY SANDS AND JESUS CHRIST

On the other hand, the lack of direct popular support in the Republic, as measurable in elections and polls, was cause for concern to Sinn Féin-IRA. People would not support violence, directly. Their ambivalence on the subject found refuge in supporting Fianna Fáil (and later also Labour, under Dick Spring). People would not vote for Sinn Féin, in the Republic. But they would respond emotionally to Republican appeals where Republicans could be seen as heirs to the Irish Catholic martyrs of old. This note was struck very forcefully, in the hunger-strikes of 1982 in which Bobby Sands and nine others fasted to death. Sands himself was a mystical Catholic-nationalist.

In 1986, in reviewing John Feehan's *Bobby Sands and the*

Tragedy of Northern Ireland (Permanent Press, Sag Harbor, New York), I wrote:

"In any case, the mystical Republicanism of Patrick Pearse, unlike the secular Republicanism of (pre-metamorphic) Tone, is an ideology of and for Catholics. Ulster Protestants reject it in all its forms, hard, soft or disguised (as in the Anglo-Irish Agreement). And so, to seek to incorporate Ulster Protestants in any kind of Irish Republic is a recipe for Holy War. Which is what is already going on, on a small scale and intermittently.

"The point is made effectively, though quite inadvertently, in John Feehan's book on Bobby Sands. Sands's self-immolation was thoroughly Pearsean, and Mr Feehan's exaltation of Sands is in a Pearsean mode (though lacking any trace of Pearse's power with words). 'The conflict has very little to do with religion', says Mr Feehan at one point, but his own metaphors and analogies and those of his hero, Sands himself, say something different. Like Pearse, Sands saw himself as one of a line of martyrs for the Republic (beginning with Tone), whose sacrifice repeats the sacrifice of Jesus Christ on the Cross. On receiving a fourteen-year-sentence for possession of arms with intent to endanger life, Sands wrote the lines:

> *The beady eyes they peered at me*
> *The time had come to be,*
> *To walk the lonely road*
> *Like that of Calvary.*
> *And take up the cross of Irishmen*
> *Who've carried liberty.*

Mr Feehan takes up this Pearsean hint, which provides the leitmotiv for his book. Near the beginning, commenting on Cardinal Hume's view that men like Sands who deliberately starve themselves to death are committing suicide, Mr Feehan comments: 'Jesus Christ could have saved his life when he came before Pilate, but he refused to do so. Did the founder of Christianity therefore commit suicide?' A few pages later on, the perceived resemblance to the founder of Christianity is more boldly suggested:

"'In the quiet evening silence of Milltown graveyard it seemed as if the Republican Movement had reached its Calvary with no Resurrection in sight, that Bobby Sands had lost and the overwhelming power of the British empire had won yet another victory.'

"The author goes on to suggest that the Resurrection duly followed in the shape of the boost given to the Republican cause by the hunger-strikers. But the clincher is in the last words of Mr Feehan's sixth and last chapter:

"'In the early hours of the morning of 5 May the immortal soul of one of the noblest young Irishmen of the twentieth century came face-to-face with his Fellow Sufferer and Maker. Bobby Sands was dead.'

"There were other fellow-sufferers, lower-case ones: the thousands who were either killed, maimed or bereaved by the devotees of the Irish Republic in Mr Sand's organisation, the Provisional IRA. Those other dead, however, being the wrong kind, are implicitly excluded from what is seen as a Celestial Tête-a-Tête.

"The effect of elevating anyone prepared to kill and die for the Republic to the status of Jesus Christ, is to annihilate, morally and spiritually, the adversaries of the Republic, whom the Republican Christ feels impelled to bump off. Those adversaries of Christ are necessarily cast in the role, if not of Antichrist himself, then of the agents, or at best the dupes, of Antichrist. They deserve no mercy, and that is exactly what they get. This is the very essence of Holy War. And Mr. Feehan shows his hero, on his last birthday, receiving with joy an ikon of Catholic Holy War: 'He was thrilled to get a picture of Our Lady from a priest in Kerry who had encouraged him to take arms for his oppressed people.' To wit, the Catholics of Northern Ireland.

"Theobald Wolfe Tone would hardly have been 'thrilled' to get such a present and such a message. But then Wolfe Tone was trying to lead people out of the seventeenth century, while Republicans of our own time have brought the seventeenth century back.

"The sole but sufficient merit of Mr Feehan's book is that it provides such authentic whiffs of the emotional mystique which keeps the IRA going, and for which some (though not all) of its members are not merely willing but anxious to die. (Nine other prisoners followed Sands's example and fasted to death). More sophisticated apologists for 'the Republican Movement' (the euphemism for the Provos and their camp-followers) like to stress the 'modern' and 'social' aspects of the movement. Mr Feehan tries to do that too – with his 'very little to do with religion' bit – but he just can't help blurting out – especially at the emotional high points – some of the obstinately archaic and numinous realities" (*New York Review of Books* 24 April 1986).

I am often reproached by moderate constitutional nationalists for "validating" or "legitimising" the Provisionals, by pointing to such continuities as exist between, for example, Pearse's mystical nationalism and that of Bobby Sands. But the IRA are certainly not looking to me (of all people) for validation or legitimacy. They have their mandate from the patriot dead, the Pearsean ghosts, and they need no outsider to keep them in mind of that. It is their *raison d'etre,* and their licence to kill.

The constitutional nationalists are in the habit of saying that it is important for democratic nationalists to hold fast to the heritage of 1916, lest it be monopolised by the Provos. This is a terrible mistake. When constitutional nationalists try to compete with the Provos for "the Republican banner" (Albert Reynolds's phrase) they end up dancing to the Provos' tune, as Mr Reynolds has been doing since December 1993. What is important is to realise what gives the Provos their strength: the cult of the dead, which is now an incubus on the living Irish people. That is why it is important to investigate and illustrate some of the workings of that cult, the better to be able to challenge it. And it must be challenged, most especially, on those manifestations of the cult which have attained the greatest prestige and authority amongst us. If you can't bring yourself to challenge Pearse, you have yourself become a carrier of the cult, an appeaser of the ghosts.

To get back to the hunger-strikes of 1982. At all those funerals – spun out over time, like the executions of 1916 – Catholic symbols were prominently in evidence: rosary-beads and crucifixes together with the tricolour, the total panoply of Catholic nationalism. This time the ghosts of 1916 were not merely walking, as in 1966, but being reinforced by new volunteer-ghosts, week after week.

Yet the impact of this series of rituals, in the Republic at least, was not as directly potent (at least in the Republic) as the organisers must have hoped. Ten years earlier, Bloody Sunday – the shooting dead by British troops of thirteen stone-throwing but unarmed Catholic nationalists in Derry in January 1972 – had evoked a passionate if short-lived popular response in the Republic. That culminated in the burning down of the British Embassy in Dublin. After that, as if sated, the popular emotion had died down. But there was no equivalent wave of popular indignation in the Republic, following the deaths of the hunger-strikers, and nothing even remotely comparable to the effects of the 1916 executions. Ghosts walked indeed, but in most people they aroused fear, and guilt about fear, rather than a blaze of indignation. Between Bloody Sunday and the death of Bobby Sands, there had been more than ten years of the Provisionals' armed struggle. The effects of that had produced a considerable revulsion in the public mind, at conscious level at least, from patriotic violence. Even the cult of 1916 had wilted a bit, since 1966. Then patriotic violence could be viewed through the comfortable haze of idealised retrospect. But since 1971 it had been in the here and now, and from the hunger-strikes it looked as if the violence had come to stay. The official commemoration, in 1991, of the seventy-fifth anniversary of the 1916 rising was much more muted than that of the fiftieth anniversary.

That was in the Republic. But the death-rituals of 1982 were powerful medicine, working for revenge, among young Catholics in Northern Ireland. As we have seen they didn't work that way in the Republic. Yet even in the Republic these rituals, in the whole context of the IRA's armed struggle, had effects that worked in the IRA's favour. At conscious level, what was evoked by all these deaths and the rituals associated with them was a longing for peace. It is not obvious that an armed struggle can be fuelled by a longing for peace, but it does sometimes work that way. Between the wars, for example, the longing for peace in Britain and France helped the Nazis to rearm with impunity. In Ireland, as well as in Britain, the general longing for an end to political violence has become the IRA's greatest asset. Partly, this is a mechanical and general phenomenon. The more you crave for peace, the more you may come to be dependent on the men of violence, who alone can supply you with that which you crave.

But there is also a reason, specific to the Catholic and nationalist context, why the longing for peace helps the IRA. Catholics and nationalists find it hard – indeed almost impossible – to conceive of a progress towards peace which is not also a progress towards the achievement of the nationalist goal: a united Ireland. This is also, of course, the goal of the IRA. Though most people strongly disapprove of the IRA's *methods*, there is general approval for a peace process, designed to attain the same objective, through non-violent means. In practice, as far as the unionist population is concerned, the peace process joins forces with the armed struggle, as part of one sustained Catholic-nationalist enterprise, intended to extort Protestant and unionist consent to that which all unionists and almost all Protestants refuse: a united Ireland.

In the period 1982-5, the longing for peace, fuelled by the hunger-strike rituals, produced a strong demand for concessions by Britain to the constitutional nationalists. Shaken by the impact of the hunger-strike deaths, particularly in America, the British Government felt a need to placate the constitutional nationalists. The result of this convergence of demand and need produced the Anglo-Irish Agreement, the greatest political victory for Catholic nationalism since the abolition (aka "prorogation") of the Stormont Parliament in 1972.

That Agreement gave the Dublin Government consultative status in the affairs of Northern Ireland, through the Anglo-Irish Intergovernmental Conference. Thus Dublin – and the SDLP, through Dublin – had now a greater share in the governance of Northern Ireland than the unionists had; quite a reversal.

The Anglo-Irish Agreement, signed at Hillsborough on 15 November 1985, was preceded and accompanied by a tremendous amount of hype about how it would "reconcile the two traditions in Ireland", "end the alienation of the minority" and so "marginalise the men of violence". Nine years' experience of the Agreement has revealed these claims for the hokum they always were. But nobody in Ireland cares about that, because nobody in Ireland ever believed those claims in the first place (except perhaps Garret FitzGerald, who has an unusual capacity for kidding himself, perhaps because he is too decent to understand dark forces in history). The reality was, and is, that the Hillsborough Agreement represents a breakthrough for Catholic nationalists over Protestant unionists. What remains, as John Hume and his followers understand, is to exploit that breakthrough until the final victory of Catholics and nationalists is attained.

In the wake of that Agreement, what has emerged is not anything remotely resembling a reconciliation of the two traditions, but rather a closing of the ranks of one tradition against the other. The "men of violence", on the Catholic and nationalist side, instead of being "marginalised" have now become integrated into a pan-Catholic and pan-nationalist consensus, along with the SDLP, the Dublin Government and the Catholic Church. This is known as "the peace process" a use of language which is the up-to-date version of the kind of hokum that preceded the Hillsborough Agreement and has now been "transcended" (a word dear to Irish nationalist discourse in the late twentieth century).

MR ADAMS AND MR HUME

The pan-nationalist peace process, as it emerged in 1993-4, is based on a dialogue, and an agreement or agreements between Gerry Adams, President of Sinn Féin, and John Hume, leader of the Social Democratic and Labour Party. The existence of an agreement – and there certainly is at least one agreement – between these two Catholic and nationalist leaders is in itself a remarkable phenomenon. Sinn Féin is an organisation pledged to support the IRA's armed struggle, and is in fact controlled by the IRA, of whose Army Council Mr Adams is generally believed to be a member. The Social Democratic and Labour Party is dedicated to peaceful change, and Mr Hume's international celebrity is based to a large extent on his eloquently expressed abhorrence of political violence. So Hume-Adams – or, as the Republican side puts it, Adams-Hume – is a bit of a puzzle. It is a puzzle that concerns us, in the context of the present study, for Hume-Adams, aka Adams-Hume, is the most conspicuous manifestation of Catholic nationalism in the middle of the last decade of the twentieth century.

So what exactly *is* Hume-Adams? So far as I know, the two leaders have made only one joint statement, which was published in the Irish Sunday newspapers on 25 April, 1993. The core of this joint statement is the following:

"We accept that the Irish people as a whole have a right to national self-determination."

That formula leaves absolutely no room for compromise between Catholics/nationalists and Protestants/unionists in Ireland. It is a classical expression of traditional Catholic Republican nationalism, always rejected and resisted by Protestants and unionists. Ireland's "right to national self-determination" is a breakthrough for the ghosts.

If that "right" is to be vindicated, it will have to be imposed on the Protestants and unionists by force. Yet this formula for civil war is the core of the Hume-Adams peace process. How come?

Part of the answer is that the original joint statement has been overlaid by a Hume-Adams folklore, circulating among moderate nationalists, and *apparently* allowing room for compromise. Thus the following appeared in a Dublin newspaper in mid-July under the heading: "Hume-Adams document":

"The democratic right to self-determination by the people of the island as a whole must be achieved and exercised *with the agreement and consent of the people of Northern Ireland*" (my italics CCO'B).[76]

I shall believe that version when I see it confirmed by Gerry Adams, in which case that confirmation will be followed immediately by the departure of Mr Adams from the Presidency of Sinn Féin, and possibly also from this world.

A President of Sinn Féin who would agree to the omission of the key-word "national", before self-determination, would be guilty of the gravest of sins and crimes: national apostasy. Mr Adams in fact, in his frequent public references to "self-determination" *always* prefaces that word with "national" and the most recent conference of the Sinn Féin party (Letterkenny, July, 1994) committed itself, as a matter of course, to the "exercise of national self-determination". And if Mr Adams, addressing his party at Letterkenny had used the formula "with the agreement and consent of the people of Northern Ireland", he would have been beaten to a pulp. The mere words "Northern Ireland" are unspeakable in a Republican context and "the people of Northern Ireland" is even worse.

I believe that phoney versions of "Hume-Adams" are part of

---

76. Quoted under the above heading in an article by Garret FitzGerald (*Irish Times* 16 July, 1994). Garret got this version from Seamus Mallon. The good faith of both these gentleman is beyond question, but the document they have been led to accept is spurious.

a general process of disinformation which led to, and followed, the Downing St Declaration of 15 December, 1993. That Declaration, with its inclusion of a (hedged) formula concerning Irish self-determination, was supposed to induce a "war-weary" IRA to agree to a "permanent cessation of violence". The Letterkenny Conference of Sinn Féin, after seven (post-Declaration) months of continuous IRA violence – and rising loyalist violence – finally gave a thumbs-down to Downing St, but reconfirmed its commitment to "the peace process", based on Adams-Hume. It also affirmed its commitment to the 1916 Proclamation of the Republic, which is incompatible with any peace except through total victory by nationalists over unionists.

In the context of the present study, what concerns us is what Adams-Hume (as I shall now call it) has to tell us about the current condition of Catholic nationalism in Ireland. And what Adams-Hume has to tell us is not good.

The best hope for peace in Northern Ireland has always been for an agreement between moderate nationalists and moderate unionists, and a common front of both against the men of violence *on both sides*: both the IRA and the loyalist paramilitaries. Such a consensus could have led to the taking, by both the Dublin and London Governments, of the necessary drastic measures – including internment of the paramilitary godfathers – against both sets of terrorists. Terrorism can never be brought to an end except by recourse to such measures.

From its beginning in 1970, under the leadership of Gerry Fitt, the SDLP genuinely sought accommodation with the unionists. Gerry Fitt's loathing of the IRA was courageously explicit and amply reciprocated. As long as he and Paddy Devlin were active in the leadership of the SDLP, there could be no question of any kind of partnership with Sinn Féin.

But after John Hume replaced Gerry Fitt in the leadership (1979) there was a change in approach. Though the rhetoric about "agreement between the two traditions" became more fluent than ever, the real objective was now to circumvent the unionists and squeeze them. The Anglo-Irish Agreement (which was above all John Hume's brainchild) was the first major triumph for this policy. The idea there, was to go over the heads of the unionists to the British, and get the latter to push the unionists in the direction that they don't want to go: that of a united Ireland ("an agreed Ireland" in Humespeak). John Hume has never abandoned the policy of using the British to squeeze the unionists. But by the late eighties, with the Anglo-Irish Agreement under his belt, Mr Hume was talking about the need to "transcend" that Agreement. The Agreement itself has been rejected (formally) by Sinn Féin, but an attempt to "transcend" it, by further movement down the nationalist agenda, might be the basis for a common front of all nationalists.

Talks between Gerry Adams and John Hume began in the late 1980's but did not immediately lead to any joint declaration. But they began again in earnest in 1992, and led to the Adams-Hume joint statement of April, 1993 (quoted above).

In theory, the Adams-Hume agreement represented a movement in the direction of peace. The reality was the opposite. *Any* joint declaration between the leader of the SDLP and the President of Sinn Féin would have automatically poisoned relations between the SDLP and all unionists. The self-determination formula adopted by the two leaders amounted to a declaration of war against unionists, and against the existence of Northern Ireland, and that formula also registered a regression on the part of the SDLP. This formula represents *what has always been the policy of Sinn Féin-IRA*. It is the classic Republican formula, dictated by the ghosts and irreversible by the living. Hume simply signed on the dotted line. In the pan-nationalist consensus that began to emerge in April, 1993, the dominant partner is Sinn Féin-IRA.

Through John Hume, the Dublin Coalition government of Albert Reynolds and Dick Spring has been drawn into this pan-nationalist and pan-Catholic alliance against the unionists. Sinn Féin-IRA have been the only beneficiaries of this alliance.

Sinn Féin was awarded (for the first time ever) access to the national broadcasting network, RTE. The Dublin Government, through the so-called "friends of Ireland" in Congress, got Gerry Adams a visa for the United States, on the plea that he was now working for peace. Once there, he worked for peace by blasting the Brits on coast-to-coast television.

The Dublin Government got nothing whatever in exchange for these concessions, but that never seemed to worry Albert Reynolds. As the IRA violence continued, month after month, in spite of the Downing St Declaration, Mr Reynolds found a formula for reconciling himself and his Government to this disconcerting aspect of the peace process. The formula consisted of a fragment wrenched out of its context from WB Yeats's "Lake Isle of Innisfree": "Peace comes dropping slow". This sounds merely inane, but it is really sinister. It is a formula for continuing to cosy up to Sinn Féin, *while Sinn Féin's masters, the IRA, keep right on killing people.* All Sinn Féin has to do, to remain on excellent terms with Dublin, is to keep on talking about peace. And in that respect, Sinn Féin is indefatigable. In his statements to the Letterkenny Conference, Gerry Adams mentioned the word "peace" no less than 33 times. No doubt this statistic was among the positive signals that Albert Reynolds received from Letterkenny: if peace comes dropping slow, 33 drops is quite a lot.

There were other positive signals. Every now and then, Gerry Adams and Albert Reynolds exchange compliments from a distance. It is rather like the courtship of birds. Mr Reynolds will pay tribute to "the sincerity of Mr Adams's commitment to peace". Mr Adams will then acknowledge "the Taoiseach's positive contribution to the peace process". So everybody is happy, except the people who continue to be murdered by Mr Adams's bosses, throughout these pacific exchanges.

It has become apparent that it is Mr Reynolds who covets the approval of Mr Adams and not *vice versa.* And this is part of the inner logic of the Republican movement. The fiercer nationalist always tends to dominate the feebler, over the whole nationalist field. But within the Republican movement, specifically, the mandate from the dead always outweighs the mandate from the living. Albert Reynolds has a mandate from the living, but he knows, in his Republican heart, that that doesn't count for much. Those whom Gerry Adams represents have the mandate from the dead, because they are, in the here and now, doing the bidding of the ghosts and supplying them with the blood they crave. In the Adams-Hume partnership, and in the Adams-Reynolds partnership, which grew out of the former, Gerry Adams is the predominant partner. He is so, because his credentials are superior, emotionally, within the Catholic-nationalist-Republican tradition, as expounded (although with some variations) by the Christian Brothers in the nineteenth century, by Irish Ireland (with its explicitly sectarian input) in the early twentieth century, by Yeats and Maud Gonne in *Cathleen ni Houlihan*, and then by Patrick Pearse, and all the varieties of Irish nationalists of later generations who claim allegiance to Pearse. You can't have Pearse without the ghosts, and you can't appease the ghosts unless you do what they want. We have Pearse's word for that.

THE MALIGN MODEL

Twenty-two years ago, I wrote a book called *States of Ireland*. In the last chapter of that book I offered two main alternative models for the future of this problem [Northern Ireland]. One of these I called "the benign model". That one need not detain us now, since it was dependent on the hypothesis that the Catholic population of Northern Ireland would repudiate the IRA. That has not happened and has never looked less like happening than in 1993-4 (after Adams-Hume). We are left, then, with the malignant model. Part of that model has already been fulfilled in practice, and something like the remainder looks increasingly probable. The "malignant model" as offered by me in 1972 opens as follows:

"The Provisional offensive will continue (possibly with a

limited 'tactical' interruption) and even escalate. It will provoke an escalating Protestant counter-offensive including the murder of prominent Catholics, followed by retaliatory murders of Protestants."

The prediction in the first sentence has already been fulfilled. That in the second sentence is being fulfilled now. After the Downing St Declaration, loyalist paramilitary murders sharply increased. The rest of the malignant model remains surmise, but it is the kind of surmise that is relevant to what we are now seeing, so it is worth while to quote.

"This will be followed by massed Protestant assaults on Catholic ghettoes. Some of these will be contained by the Army, some will break through. Where breakthroughs occur, the only defence the Catholics will have will be the IRA. In these conditions the IRA regains control over the ghettoes in question and can continue its activities indefinitely. The British Army comes under armed attack from both communities. With increasing casualties and no solution in sight, the British public clearly favours a policy of withdrawal. A British Government announces its agreement to the unity of Ireland, for which it receives many telegrams of congratulation from America, and urgent private messages of alarm from Dublin. The British Government, indicating that the policing of a united Ireland is a matter for the Irish Government, terminates its peace-keeping role and begins a withdrawal of its troops. Mass meetings of loyalists in Belfast acclaim 'no surrender'. An official mission from Dublin to negotiate a 'federal solution' is unable to move outside the Catholic areas of Belfast. Armed Loyalists move en masse into these ghettoes to get rid of the IRA once and for all, to lynch the Dublin emissaries, and to punish the Catholics generally. Thousands of Catholics are killed and scores of thousands fly south in terror: thus the water and the fish go down the drain together, from the eastern part of Northern Ireland. In the western and southern parts, Catholics start killing Protestants, and Protestants fly north and east. With or without orders from the Dublin government, the Irish army takes over in

Newry, Derry and Strabane, and surrounding Catholic areas. Its efforts to penetrate the Protestant hinterland are held off, or beaten back."

(There follows a passage about an appeal to the United Nations, but as this was written in Cold War conditions it is no longer applicable, in the form written. But UN intervention remains exceedingly unlikely). The rest of the malignant model follows:

"Ireland would be left, once more, with two States, but of even more virulent shades of green and orange than before. The Orange State would be smaller than before – probably about four counties – but would be homogeneously Protestant, without the tiniest Catholic crack or crevice for a new IRA to take root in. The Green State with its massive ingestion of embittered and displaced Ulster Catholics, would be an uncongenial environment for Protestants, most of whom would probably leave. A tiny minority would probably remain in order to proclaim from time to time how well treated they were and how non-sectarian everything was compared with the terrible conditions prevailing in the North.

"Both states would be under right-wing governments, scruffily militarist and xenophobe in character. The principal cultural activities would be funerals, triumphal parades, commemorations, national days of mourning, and ceremonies of rededication to the memory of those who died for Ireland/for Ulster."

I wish that the above could reasonably be treated, in 1994, as some kind of morbid fantasy. But I find, as I look at it, twenty-two years after those words were written, that such dire predictions look more probable now, by far, than they did then. When those words were written, the IRA offensive had been sustained for less than two years. By now, it is twenty-three.

At the centre of the new pan-Catholic and pan-nationalist consensus is a pair of exceptionally resourceful and versatile politicians: John Hume, the SDLP leader, and Gerry Adams, President of Sinn Féin-IRA. As is usual in these matters, there is a theory about the Hume-Adams alliance, and there is a reality, quite at variance with the theory.

In late 1993, Mr Hume convinced the Dublin Government that the IRA was "war-weary", and was prepared to agree to "a permanent cessation of violence", provided the British would agree to some formula with "self-determination" in it. Mr Hume had, apparently acquired this conviction from Mr Adams. Albert Reynolds succeeded in conveying something of this conviction to John Major and the result was the Downing Street Declaration of 15 December 1993, in which the only new feature was a favourable (though hedged) reference to Irish self-determination. This advance on the Anglo-Irish Agreement (as it was from a nationalist point of view) was expected to lead to early peace, and received the same extravagant ululations of acclaim from the media as had accompanied the Anglo-Irish Agreement.

After the Declaration, as before, the supposedly war-weary IRA kept up its armed struggle (subject always to tactical ceasefires). Sinn Féin for its part, asked for "clarifications" meaning further concessions to the nationalists (which would of course have to be followed by still further concession-clarifications, right up to a United Ireland).

The Reynolds-Spring Government, at the time of the publication of the Declaration, put out the word that if the IRA did not promptly accord that "permanent cessation of violence", they were going to clamp down on the IRA in a big way. There was even talk of internment but that one faded quickly. Fairly soon, the whole idea of a clamp-down faded. After several months of continuing armed struggle, from the time of the Declaration, there was no longer any talk at all of any clampdown. Mr Reynolds just kept on with "Peace comes dropping slow", a slogan that grew increasingly sinister the longer the violence continued. The Government seemed to be quite happy with a situation in which the peace process of the constitutional nationalists plus Sinn Féin might continue indefinitely in parallel with the armed struggle of the physical force nationalists, both being directed towards the same ultimate objective, a United Ireland. This is quite near to the Michael Collins policy of 1922: peace with Britain combined with deniable encouragement to war against the Protestants of Northern Ireland. We are acting out in Ireland the Orwellian slogan, "Peace Means War".

The theory is that Mr Hume has been pressing Mr Adams to press the IRA into agreeing to a permanent cessation of violence, and that Mr Adams is now trying hard to do this. If Mr Adams is to succeed in this laudable enterprise, he needs help from the London and Dublin Governments. Some help was forthcoming in the Joint Declaration of 15 December 1993, but this is not quite enough. A bit more is needed, and a bit more time, before Mr Adams will be able to deliver peace. So much for the theory.

The reality is that Mr Adams remains what he has long been: the chief political servant of the IRA. What he means by "peace" is what the IRA has always meant: the condition that will prevail after the British withdraw and the Protestants are beaten into submission. The advantage of Hume-Adams, for the Adams side of the partnership, is that it gives Sinn Féin-IRA unprecedented leverage and a degree of legitimacy never before accorded to them (including, as I have said, for the first time in the history of the Irish State, access for Sinn Féin to the Irish national broadcasting system). By holding out the hope of peace while continuing to wage war the IRA are installing themselves securely in the large zone of ambivalence, in relation to political violence, that exists within Catholic nationalism.

It is instructive to compare, on the one hand the progress made in the talks on the future of Northern Ireland (comprising *inter alia* talks between unionists and constitutional nationalists) and, on the other, the talks between the constitutional nationalists (SDLP) and the physical force nationalists (Sinn Féin).

The talks between unionists and nationalists (including the Dublin Government) were spun out over more than two years and never got anywhere. The unionist side wanted the Anglo-

Irish Agreement replaced. The nationalist side wanted it "transcended" by which they meant, replaced by something even more obnoxious to unionists – because closer to a United Ireland – than the Anglo-Irish Agreement is. Failing "transcendence", the nationalist side would offer the unionist side nothing that they wanted. If – as nationalists always claim – they want better relations with the unionists, they could have attained that end – even with the Anglo-Irish Agreement still in place – by willingness to amend Articles 2 and 3 of the Irish Constitution. It is the combination of the Anglo-Irish Agreement with the territorial claim in Articles 2 and 3 that unionists find intolerable. The maintenance of the territorial claim – now ruled to be a "constitutional imperative" by the Irish Supreme Court – nullifies the proviso in the Anglo-Irish Agreement that there can be no united Ireland without the assent of a majority of the population of Northern Ireland. In the Republic of Ireland, that proviso only applies as far as it may be found compatible with Articles 2 and 3 as interpreted by the Supreme Court. And the Supreme Court's doctrine that "the reintegration of the national territory" is "a constitutional imperative" is an absolutist position. It allows no room for choice on the part of any kind of majority in any part of the national territory, which is the whole island *de jure*, and must be reintegrated *de facto*, according to a Supreme Court appointed by governments chosen by the electorate of Twenty-six Counties, exclusively.

Knowing all that, the nationalist side showed no willingness to amend Articles 2 and 3. The basic nationalist position, since the hardening that set in in 1969, ending the relative *détente* of the Lemass years, has been to keep the Articles in place, while implying that they might be changed, if the unionists conceded enough. By the summer of 1994, this policy took the official form of an offer by the Taoiseach, Albert Reynolds, to initiate amendment of Articles 2 and 3 provided "cross-border institutions set up with executive powers" are agreed. In other words, the unionists could get rid of something to which they strongly objected only by accepting something to which they are known to object even more strongly. Predictably, the unionists refused this offer, which was made in order to be refused, thus safeguarding the Articles against British pressure for their amendment. Actually the nationalist programme is to maintain the Articles in force, until the unionists cave in, at which point the Articles will no longer be needed, the "constitutional imperative" contained in them having been fulfilled. Defending the retention of Articles 2 and 3 before a meeting of the British-Irish Interparliamentary Body in Dublin in the last week of April 1994 the Taoiseach Albert Reynolds had said that to remove these Articles in isolation "would give the greatest boost to the Provisional IRA you or I have ever seen. It would be handing over the banner of republicanism to the IRA".

So the Provisionals have a veto on constitutional change in the Republic. Articles 2 and 3, with the irredentist territorial claim to Northern Ireland, constitute the banner of Republicanism. Fianna Fáil and the IRA, as branches of the broad Republican movement, each hold on to a corner of that banner. The Irish Labour Party is not entitled to a corner of the sacred banner, not being part of the Republican movement. Yet Labour, under Dick Spring, is content to trudge behind the banner, and keep in office a Government which is happy to hug its corner of it, while the IRA holds the other.

The notion of that banner explains a lot. A democratically-elected Prime Minister is connected to the terrorist wing of "the Republican Movement" through the notion of a common banner, as well as in other ways. Since Fianna Fáil will not let go of the banner, Fianna Fáil is being carried along by its sinister but more dynamic partner – with its more secure grip on the banner – in the direction of civil war. The bond between Fianna Fáil, on the one hand, and Sinn Féin-IRA on the other is by no means confined to the metaphor of the banner. There are rites and cults common to the whole "Republican Movement". Fianna Fáil and Provisional Sinn Féin-IRA annually repair in June (though on different days) to the grave of Wolfe Tone at Bodenstown, there to testify to their Republican faith.The Tone they honour is, of course, Pearse's Tone, not the original child of the Enlightenment. The sense of shared values, around the cult of Bodenstown, helped to prepare the way for the current alliance between Albert Reynolds and Gerry Adams. Even when the "peace process" beginning with the Downing St Declaration was obviously in tatters (by the second half of 1994) the cosy relationship between Albert Reynolds and Gerry Adams subsisted. At the Letterkenny Conference of Sinn Féin (24 July, 1994) the Downing St Declaration was rejected (as an inadequate basis for peace) but Albert Reynolds was praised for his contribution to the peace process. Not to be outdone, Mr Reynolds claimed to detect "positive signals" coming from Letterkenny. Nobody else did, but Albert Reynolds is Taoiseach. His comment reassured Sinn Féin-IRA. They can now safely continue their armed struggle (complete with occasional conditional and temporary ceasefires) while staying in comfortable cahoots with the Dublin Government.

The relationship now established between Gerry Adams and Albert Reynolds is the outstanding contemporary example of the "differential" we have had occasion to consider in other contexts. Both men hear the ghosts: Mr Reynolds faintly, Mr Adams strongly. In these conditions, the one who hears them strongly will dominate his partner. If we think in terms of a common "Republican Movement" embracing both Fianna Fáil and Sinn Féin-IRA (the banner bit) the senior member in that partnership is Mr Adams, not Mr Reynolds. The more Mr Adams flatters Mr Reynolds (as he now frequently does) the more power over Mr Reynolds he can exercise. Mr Reynolds knows in his heart that Mr Adams represents the *real* Republican movement: the people who are fighting for Ireland now. Fianna Fáil has long been accused of having "sold out" by those who firmly grasp the other corner of that coveted banner. Courtesy of the peace, Fianna Fáil have now achieved a degree of acceptance by the real Republican movement, and this warms their hearts. They are, to an acceptable degree, doing the thing the ghost is asking of them. Fianna Fáil has come in from the Republican cold.

It's a bad look out for the rest of us. And it is no wonder, in these conditions that the cycle of tit-for-tat sectarian murders should be speeding up amid the conflicting hopes and fears of the delusive peace process. Having the unionists at a disadvantage, the nationalists fully intended, and intend, to keep them that way. This is understandable in the light of history. But it is altogether incompatible with the benign and oecumenical rhetoric which is forever on the lips of consititutional nationalists, whenever it is a question of vague generalities, and not of specifics, like Articles 2 and 3.

Those things being so, the talks involving unionist and nationalists ended deadlocked. It was quite otherwise with the talks between constitutional nationalists and physical force nationalists (Hume-Adams). These eventuated in April, 1993, in that Joint Statement, in which Mr Hume and Mr Adams together reasserted "the right of the people of Ireland to national self-determination". This is a classical nationalist position, fully compatible with Articles 2 and 3, and altogether incompatible with any form of unionism or with the existence of Northern Ireland.

Taken together, then, what these two sets of talks both express is the determination of Irish Catholic irredentist nationalism to get back control over the territory which has been held for centuries by Irish Protestant unionists. The constitutionalists among the Catholic nationalists disclaim irredentism, but their bad faith, in this particular, is exposed by their refusal to change the irredentist part of the Constitution: Articles 2 and 3. The constitutional nationalists – especially Mr Hume and Cardinal Daly – constantly wax eloquent on the need to take the unionist position into account and to seek unionist consent for necessary changes. But their actions and refusals – as over Articles 2 and 3 – say something different. In reality, they agree with Sinn Féin that "the unionist veto" must go. Mr Hume likes to imply (for British and wet nationalist consumption) that "self-determination" might include some kind of self-determination for unionists, but Mr Adams has never corroborated that interpretation and Mr Adams is now the business end of Hume-Adams.

The Catholic Hierarchy was happy with "the peace process", both because of its putatively eirenic character, and because of its underlying but deniable anti-Protestant thrust. Indeed, the Church itself was very much part of this peculiar peace process, as appears from a statement issued by Cardinal Cahal Daly, Primate of All Ireland, on 18 February, 1994. The statement was entitled "Peace: Why Wait? An appeal to Sinn Féin." The statement contains just one paragraph which unequivocally condemns political violence but the paragraph does not apply to the IRA. The paragraph runs:

"The continuing murderous campaign by loyalist gunmen against nationalist public representatives and against the nationalist and Catholic community in general is unspeakably evil and should be condemned by everyone, regardless of their political affiliation. There should be no attempt to lend spurious justification to this campaign as a response to political developments."

The Primate did not, at any point in that quite lengthy statement, allude to any murderous campaign by Catholics and nationalists against Protestants and unionists, nor did he there characterise any form of Catholic or nationalist activity as unspeakably evil, or evil at all. He appealed to Sinn Féin, on grounds of expediency, and in respectful even deferential tones, to desist from their campaign. All the moral condemnation was reserved for the Protestant side. The Cardinal had in the past strongly condemned IRA violence, and after his appeal for peace was (implicitly) rejected by Sinn Féin-IRA at Letterkenny in July, he again strongly reproved the IRA. His personal detestation of all political violence is not in doubt and the marked imbalance in his February appeal has to be seen as tactical. It was, however, regrettable on the part of one to whom people look for instruction on moral issues, untempered by political tactics.

At one time, I had hoped that Cardinal Daly's concern for

peace might lead him to call for a review of Articles 2 and 3 of the Republic's Constitution. When he became Cardinal I wrote to him to express this hope, and after congratulating him I argued that to lay claim to territory, while taking no account of the wishes of the inhabitants of the territory in question, is both immoral in itself, and conducive to violent conflict. I received, by way of answer, a courteous letter from the palace, thanking me for my congratulations, and not adverting in any way to my argument. It was a civil epistolary equivalent to Cardinal Conway's gesture with my copy of the Constitution.

One has to conclude that the Church, like the Supreme Court, is behind the irredentist claim and is part of the pan-nationalist consensus for the squeezing of the Northern Ireland Protestants.

The Cardinal's blessing is undoubtedly of service to this bogus peace process, and therefore to the people to whom he appeals, Sinn Féin-IRA. But the holy war, now covered by the cloak of the peace process, does not depend on the blessing of the institutional Church, although the Church is helpful in bolstering the credibility of that cloak.

The doctrinal authority of the Catholic Church has been visibly waning in Ireland in the last quarter, and especially the last decade, of the twentieth century. I once toyed with the thought that a post-Catholic Ireland would free itself from sacral nationalism. I now see this to be a fallacy. Religious nationalism in Ireland has never depended on the *authority* of the Church, and has sometimes run counter to it (as in 1798 and 1922). It derives from Irish history, both as actually experienced and as subsequently expounded (eg by the Christian Brothers). It consists, not of doctrinal formulae, but of feelings clustering around symbols and epiphanies. In any Irish debate about the IRA, you can feel its presence, impalpable but pervasive, inflecting the views and language of people who are not conscious of being at all affected by it. It manifests itself through irrational convictions such as the belief – widely held at the end of 1993 and the beginning of

1994 and still lingering in late 1994 – that an association of hardened killers still in the killing business is really motivated by a longing for peace.

In any culture, the convergence of religion and nationalism is dangerous. The Irish form of the convergence has been less lethal, so far at least, than some others at some times: as for example, between Hindus and Muslims, or Serbs and Croats. But the Irish convergence is as potentially destructive as those others. Religious nationalism is no longer being taught in the schools in the directly inflammatory way it was once taught by the Brothers. But it seems to have ways of propagating itself outside the schools, in homes, in the media, obliquely. We have not done with it yet, and I feel in my bones that we may never have done with it. Not in my lifetime certainly, and probably not in the lifetime of any of my children.

The pressure of religious nationalism has been increasing throughout 1993 and into 1994. The violent and non-violent kind, now working more and more closely together, constitute a formidable and versatile combined force.

This pan-nationalist alliance is able to generate increased support in America for pressure on Britain, in the supposed interests of peace. Previous governments in Dublin had warned friends of Ireland in Congress not to give any aid or comfort to Sinn Féin-IRA. As a result of those warnings those Irish-Americans who are interested in the affairs of Ireland were divided. The IRA had its allies – in bodies such as Noraid, the Caucus and the Ancient Order of Hibernians – while senior figures in Congress heeded the warning from Dublin. But now those warnings have lapsed. Sinn Féin has become respectable, as part of "the peace process" (aka, after Letterkenny, "the quest for peace"). In these conditions, increasing American pressure on Britain to "create the conditions for peace", by further concessions to the nationalist agenda, may be expected. All this pressure is of course generated by Irish-American Catholics who identify only with the Catholics in Ireland, and who see Ulster Protestants as having no legitimate existence in the island of Ireland. The pressure so generated will increase in the probable event of a temporary and conditional IRA ceasefire. In such a case, President Clinton is likely to redeem his campaign promise of a Peace Envoy for Northern Ireland, thus greatly increasing American pressure on Britain to comply with the Irish nationalist agenda.

I fear it may not be many years before the British yield to the pan-nationalist pressure, with its American backing, to the extent of disengaging from Northern Ireland. But the British will not – as constitutional nationalists and their American leaders fondly hope – hang around before they go, trying to "persuade" the unionists to give in, nor will they try to crush their resistance to Irish unity. If the British decide to go, they will just go, and quite quickly – as from India, in 1947, as from Palestine in 1948 – leaving both sets of natives to fight it out. That is the direction in which our particular combination of religion and nationalism is now blindly impelling us.

Granted the state of mutual hostility and fear which already exists in Northern Ireland – a condition bound to become hideously inflamed amid the confusion and panic produced by impending British withdrawal – it is certain that withdrawal would be followed by Bosnian conditions with both sides practising ethnic cleansing, though without using such words. Most of the materials for that catastrophe are now in place, and our political leaders play with these materials, in their rhetorical posturings, without any apparent awareness of the horrors they may bring down on all of us.

In a collection of essays on related subjects (*God Land: Reflections on Religion and Nationalism,* Harvard, 1988), I was looking at certain interactions of religion and nationalism, at other times and in other places, with the kind of pleasurable fascination with which one may contemplate complex and often paradoxical phenomena which do not affect one personally. But as I contemplate the gathering convergence between religion and nationalism in our own island at this time, I feel I am looking at an x-ray plate containing evidence of a terminal disease.

This is not so for sure. As we have seen, religion and nationalism have sometimes converged and then diverged again in the course of Irish history (and have also fluctuated wildly in intensity). They are now converging, in a blandly-camouflaged pincer movement, impudently labelled "peace process," or "quest for peace" directed against the religious and political minority in the island of Ireland. There may be some new mutation, perhaps following an escalation of violence, provoking a new divergence. All we can say for sure is that the danger of civil war increases with every day this insidious pressure is kept up, including as it does the "armed struggle" of the IRA, condoned by the Dublin Government, under the Reynolds slogan, "Peace comes dropping slow", and encouraged by a pan-nationalist consensus, including the Dublin Government, the IRA and the Catholic Church around the territorial claim expressed in the constitutional imperative of Articles 2 and 3.

In the pleasant, everyday life of the Republic of Ireland, where I mostly live, it hardly seems possible that things can really be like that. This is a good-humoured, humorous people for the most part, with an increasingly easygoing attitude towards their religion, and a nationalism that seems far from fanatical. People seem far more interested in sport and pastimes, in food and drink and in money, than they are interested in Northern Ireland. Few of them are anti-British, most of them are indeed mildly pro-British. These are not wild Serbs or furious Croats. They are tolerant, willing to live and let live in most matters. (They tolerate me, for example).

Yet there are symptoms of other forces at work beneath the placid surface, in the ancestral dark. Articles 2 and 3 remain acceptable. The position of the constitutional nationalists is widely approved and their alliance, beginning in 1993, with the physical-force nationalists has been widely condoned on the seductive theory that it is really an alliance for peace. In the media, otherwise intelligent people treat the transparently bogus oecumenism of the constitutional nationalists with an outward respect which reflects concurrence in the underlying unavowed hostility to Protestants and unionists.

Above all, there appears to be almost universal assent to the notion that it is the proper task of nationalist representatives to squeeze the unionists, and get others to squeeze them in the general direction of a united Ireland. Most Catholic nationalists are not anti-British. Yet a quiet sustained *absent-minded* hostility to the Ulster unionist Protestants comes through in usually coded forms. The message to the unionists – never explicit but always inplacably implied is: "Why should we listen to you? You have no right to be *here*".

As I read certain Dublin newspapers, day after day, I think of my Epigraph and of Ibsen's Alving: "I just have to pick up a newspaper, and it's as if I could see the ghosts slipping between the lines". "Slipping between the lines", is perfect. There is nothing ghostly, or atavistic, or overtly irrational in the actual language used. The nationalism on view is moderate in tone, and apparently in substance also. It is just the basic assumptions that are dictated by the ghosts: that we must keep on pressing in the direction of a united Ireland, and that such pressure, of its nature, represents progress towards peace, however strong the indications to the contrary may be. These propositions are not argued. Nobody asks: "What do we want a united Ireland *for*?" Nobody asks: "How much blood is a united Ireland *worth*?" The propositions are just *there*: inherited assumptions, sacral premises, treasured axioms of the tribe. The ghosts that slip between the lines will tolerate no alternative assumptions, premises or axioms.

Nor can the language of this haunted discourse ever safely be taken at its face value. Thus, most nationalists say that there can be no united Ireland without the consent of a majority in Northern Ireland. Polls show this. But polls also show that most people in the Republic reject the idea of a "unionist veto" over unity. And in practice, the pressure in the direction of a united Ireland produces progress by instalments, *without* unionist consent. The largest instalment, the Anglo-Irish Agreement of 15 November, 1985, was obtained without any consultation whatever with unionists, and the nationalist strategy aims at further instalments – for example "cross-border institutions with executive powers" – to be obtained by negotiation with Britain over the heads of the unionists. Yet this process is presented as if it constitutes a quest for accommodation with unionists. The Anglo-Irish Agreement is itself a case in point.

The hype about that Agreement should not have fooled a bright teenager, moderately familiar with the actual situation. But the Irish media generally treated the stuff about reconciling the two traditions, and so on, with marked respect.

On the Irish nationalist side, the unctuous talk about reconciling the two traditions masked satisfaction that our side – Irish Catholic nationalists – had scored against the Protestant unionists. But satisfaction over that had to be dressed up as satisfaction of a more modern and high-minded character, with no overt trace of the atavistic gloating that was really there. The same is true today of the apparently unquenchable welcome for the implausible Downing St "peace process". As I take note, thankfully enough, of the tolerance generally prevalent in our society, but then get these recurring disquieting sightings of something different, under the tolerance, certain lines of WH Auden come to mind:

> *Behind each peaceable home-loving eye*
> *The private massacres are taking place*
> *All women, Jews, the human race*

The slow but powerful current of territorial aggressivity beneath the bland surface of life in the Republic of Ireland suggests a strongly irredentist subconscious, historically formed, and developed along Christian Brothers and Pearsean lines. God Land is in there, deep down. It whispers to us in the watches of the night. Our ancestors, faithful to God and Mary, once held this whole island, before the foreign heretic took it from us by force and treachery. By God's will, we have got most of it back and we are going to get the rest of it back. Any blood that is shed in the process is regrettable but is not our fault. It is *their* fault, for withholding what is rightfully ours.

Very few people talk on anything like those lines, these days, or consciously think such thoughts. But that is how the choreography of religion and nationalism is working, through a variety of subtly intricate ritual-political dances in misleadingly modern dress.

I should like to close on a more hopeful note, but as I contemplate the wreckage of my poor "benign model", the words die on my lips. We are hearing the Pearsean ghosts, at varied but increasing volumes, demanding "very big things, and they must be appeased, whatever the cost".

POSTSCRIPT

On 31 August, 1994, the Provisional IRA announced "a complete cessation of military operations". This was immediately hailed by Dublin politicians and the nationalist media as if it were equivalent (which it obviously is not) to the acceptance of the "permanent cessation of violence" for which the Downing Street Declaration had called. At the same time, the same politicians and commentators hinted that the "permanent cessation" might not be all that permanent, if the British Government failed to "respond" to it promptly by "peace dividends", meaning large concessions to IRA demands, and further movement down the nationalist agenda. To accelerate these concessions – which are also urged by the Clinton administration – Sinn Féin immediately started to apply an "unarmed strategy" consisting of street protests, direct action by civilians, and civil disobedience. The security forces cannot seriously attempt to resist the "unarmed strategy" without "endangering the ceasefire", and thus they risk becoming the helpless butts of mobs of nationalist youths. The unionist population will be witnessing a tripartite phenomenon, consisting of: increased political pressure against them, on London from Dublin, backed by Washington; a determined and well-supported effort by Sinn Féin to reduce Northern Ireland to anarchy; and, finally, the apparent impotence of the security forces, shown by their failure to control the Sinn Féin mobs.

In these conditions, increased violence from loyalist paramilitaries seems certain. The IRA are counting on this. It will enable them to return to the armed struggle, in the role of defenders of the [Catholic] people. The loyalists alone, and not the IRA at all, will be blamed by most nationalists, and many others, for the return of violence, and the dashing of the high hopes around the IRA "cessation" of 31 August 1994.

I had finished *Ancestral Voices* before the announcement of the cessation, and I have not revised the text in any way, following that announcement. I have merely added this postscript. I had foreseen (pp. 186, 190) "conditional and temporary ceasefires" complementing the armed struggle. The "cessation" of 31 August is just one such ceasefire, and marks a continuation of the armed struggle, by other means, for the moment.

The squeeze of the Ulster Protestants by the pan-Catholic and pan-nationalist consensus continues. The consensus is more assured and confident after the "cessation" even than it was before. The nationalist euphoria, after August 31, even exceeds the previous peaks in this kind: November, 1985 (the Anglo-Irish Agreement) and December 1993 (the Downing Street Declaration). Leaders of both Church and State contribute to the euphoria. Cardinal Daly, Archbishop of Armagh and Primate of All Ireland, and Dr Desmond Connell, Archbishop of Dublin and Primate of Ireland, concelebrated the cessation, as it were, along with the Taoiseach and the Tanaiste. The celebration was about peace, and would have been proper had there been peace, or any real movement towards peace. But the peace dreamed of, both by Church and State, is as always the peace of nationalist assumptions: the peace that is invariably ultimately identical with the triumph of nationalism and the coming of a united Ireland.

The only road to *that* kind of peace in our time is through civil war, and that is the direction in which the IRA is now guiding the peace process. After the ceasefire, the process is speeding up, through the combination of external pressure on Britain, the IRA's "unarmed strategy" and loyalist responses to that pressure and that strategy. Things are not better than they were before the ceasefire. They are worse.